MW00812611

Straight Talk about
South Carolina
Divorce Law

Straight Talk about
South Carolina
Divorce Law

Robert N. Rosen

Charleston   London

History
PRESS

Published by The History Press
Charleston, SC 29403
www.historypress.net

Copyright © 2007 by Robert N. Rosen
All rights reserved

Photos courtesy of istockphoto.com

First published 2007

Manufactured in the United Kingdom

ISBN 978.1.59629.316.8

Library of Congress Cataloging-in-Publication Data

Rosen, Robert N., 1947-
Straight talk about South Carolina divorce law / Robert N. Rosen.
p. cm.
ISBN 978-1-59629-316-8 (alk. paper)
1. Divorce--Law and legislation--South Carolina. 2. Separation
(Law)--South Carolina. 3. Husband and wife--South Carolina. 4. Domestic
relations--South Carolina. I. Title.
KFS1900.R67 2007
346.75701'66--dc22
                                2007035244

Notice: The information in this book is true and complete to the best of our knowledge.
It is offered without guarantee on the part of the author or The History Press. The
reader should not rely on this book for legal advice. The author and The History Press
disclaim all liability in connection with the use of this book.

All rights reserved. No part of this book may be reproduced or transmitted in any form
whatsoever without prior written permission from the publisher except in the case of
brief quotations embodied in critical articles and reviews.

Contents

Foreword

Judge Bill Donelan, whose judgeship was devoted exclusively to deciding contested divorce cases in Richland County, was no Oliver Wendell Holmes. But he was a fair-minded judge and a thoroughly decent human being. He was one of the best judges I ever practiced before, and I have never forgotten how nice he was to me when I was a young lawyer. When he retired from the bench, the Bar Association had a small lunch for him and presented him with an engraved desk set, which included, as I recall, a mechanical pencil and a ballpoint pen. As is customary at such events, several members of the Bar got up and praised Judge Donelan elaborately for his lifetime of public service. When the time came for him to respond, he said simply, "I don't deserve all this. But, on the other hand, I have a bad case of rheumatoid arthritis in my right knee, and I don't deserve that either."

Judge Donelan was too gracious on that occasion to call attention to a far greater burden he had long suffered: for the better part of four decades, he had been condemned to devote his entire professional life to living and working among people who were in the throes of the greatest disaster that can befall most people. I refer, of course, to husbands and wives involved in divorces.

Even under the most civilized of circumstances, divorce is a horrible experience for most people. Divorce cases involve the very essence of the human experience: love, sex and money. Life presents few larger problems. Innocent children are often involved. Cruelty is commonplace. It is no wonder that divorce cases are fraught with human emotion like few other matters that come before a court for a decision. But that's not all. One of the main reasons a divorce is such a horrible experience is that most husbands and wives have no idea what's happening to them, and their lawyers are either unable or unwilling to take the time to explain.

Robert Rosen is not only one of America's premier divorce lawyers, he is also a gifted writer, with at least four widely read books to his credit. He renders an invaluable public service by this book. He explains, in a readily understandable way, exactly how every facet of the divorce process works. Of equal importance, he also explains the reason for each step in the process. Once husbands and wives come to the understanding he brings to the process, I am convinced they will be relieved of a major cause of their pain and suffering. Everybody involved in a divorce, or even considering a divorce, should read what he has written, cover to cover. If only this book had been available earlier, untold misery among husbands and wives involved in divorces could have been avoided, and Judge Donelan could have had a happier life.

Alexander M. Sanders
Former Chief Judge
South Carolina Court of Appeals

Introduction

This is a true story: When I was a young lawyer, the Family Court in Charleston was located at the Old Citadel building on Marion Square downtown. It was a ramshackle building and the courtrooms were dingy and makeshift. I went to court for a hearing on behalf of a young woman whose daughter had been forcibly taken away from her at gunpoint by her estranged husband, a career criminal. She retained my law firm to regain custody of her daughter. The thought of going into an unsecured courtroom to take custody of a child away from a criminal was not very appetizing. I mentioned to the judge that I thought everyone ought to be searched. (This took place in the 1970s, before all of the present-day security measures were in place.) I explained that I was concerned about someone getting shot. The judge became extremely angry, whipped out a revolver from his desk drawer and said, "The only one gonna do any shootin' in this courtroom is gonna be me." This was not particularly reassuring.

We have come a very long way in the Family Court system in South Carolina in the last thirty years. The quality, temperament and professionalism of the judges, as well as the expertise of the lawyers, have increased dramatically. Of course, divorce has also become commonplace. "I've never been married," Elayne Boosler quipped, "but I tell people that I am divorced so they won't think something is wrong with me."

This book is written for those who want to know how divorce and family law cases are actually handled and resolved in South Carolina. It is a practical and realistic overview of how lawyers, experts, mediators and Family Court judges operate and decide what happens in divorce, custody and matrimonial cases. This book does not offer legal advice. Every case is different. This book offers general descriptions, basic concepts and key points to consider if the reader or a friend or relative is involved in a matrimonial dispute in South Carolina. People getting divorced or involved in custody, separation or marital litigation need lawyers, preferably competent family law specialists, to advise them.

"Family law" is a phrase that encompasses legal issues arising from divorce, separation, custody disputes, child support, property division, alimony, termination of parental rights, adoption, child abuse, Department of Social Services cases, common-law marriage and prenuptial agreements, among many other matters. Family law generally does not refer to damage suits arising out of marital discord, such as suits for assault, defamation and transmission of sexually transmitted diseases.

Of course, the best advice from an experienced divorce lawyer is to reconcile with your spouse, stay married and stay out of Family Court. "Never go to bed mad," Phyllis Diller advised, "stay up and fight." Many a wise man has told me over the years, "It's cheaper to keep her." Many a wise woman has told me, "In our family we don't divorce our men—we bury them."

But if the marriage counselor, psychologist, pastoral counselor, family and friends have failed; if there is physical or emotional abuse; if the children are grown and you must have a new life; if your spouse has run off with another or loves alcohol or drugs more than you; or for a myriad of other reasons divorce or separation is a reality, here is straight talk about family law in South Carolina from a lawyer who has lived and breathed it for over thirty years.

This book is intended for the curious, educated layperson who wants to know what the law of divorce is and how it works in practice. I have cited actual published, that is, "reported," South Carolina appellate cases in the text (e.g., *Johnson v. Johnson*) so that those readers who wish to know more may do so. In order to find a published case, one can find the citation *Johnson v. Johnson*, 372 S.E. 2d. 107 (Court of Appeals 1988) at the end of the book in the Table of Cases and use the citation to find some of the more recent cases on the internet at www.sccourts.org, www.scstatehouse.net, www.cornell.edu or www.judicial.state.sc.us. All cases can be found in law books at public libraries or courthouses. The cases and some statutes cited in this book can also be found at my website, www.straighttalkscdivorce.com.

A word of caution, however: lawyers go to law school for three years to understand how the law works, and then they practice it for many more years. One cannot rely on one case or a random reading of cases and statutes to arrive at the correct answer. There is an old saying in the law that "he who represents himself has a fool for a client."

No one should get divorced without legal advice from a competent lawyer. The consequences can be devastating. For example, if your divorce is not valid, you remain legally married to your "former" spouse (even if you think you are remarried), who will inherit one third or maybe even one half of your estate on your death and who has the right to sue in the event you are killed in a car wreck or other accident. Your "former" spouse may also be entitled to all of your retirement benefits, life insurance and social security payments. Paying legal fees may not be pleasant, but usually it is a wise investment.

Therefore, if you or a loved one is involved in a domestic dispute, find the right lawyer by asking your friends, other lawyers, business associates, people whom you trust and those who have had a successful experience with a particular lawyer or law firm.

I asked a few colleagues to read portions of this book and I want to thank Professor John Freeman, Bob Stevens, Pam Deal and especially Diane Current for their kind assistance and advice. Expert mediator Mark O. Andrews also contributed his expertise.

Chapter 1

How the System Works

The difference between divorce and legal separation is that a legal separation gives a husband time to hide his money.

—Attributed to Johnny Carson

My toughest fight was with my first wife.

—Muhammad Ali

Marital Litigation

Divorce is a legal proceeding. It involves two parties who are dissolving a legally recognized partnership and, like any two partners, the parties can settle their differences or resort to the courts. In the best of all possible worlds, divorcing spouses can settle their differences; a lawyer for one of them can write an agreement and have the agreement approved by the Family Court, which approval is required to render a marital agreement legally enforceable.

But in most cases, one party possesses greater financial resources; the other party is not aware of all the financial details; the parties may disagree on custody arrangements; and usually one party is emotionally upset, if not shattered, by the separation. Thus, there is the need for lawyers, counselors, mediators and judges in the resolution of a divorce case.

Straight Talk about South Carolina Divorce Law

Most people are mystified by the court system, but the Family Court system in South Carolina is straightforward. The powers of the Family Court include exclusive authority (jurisdiction) over marital litigation, domestic relations matters, divorce, custody of children, termination of parental rights and many other family matters. The court has the power to grant divorces, alimony (support) to a spouse on a temporary or a permanent basis, support for children, a division (apportionment) of marital property, issue restraining orders and injunctions, join such parties as are necessary to effect its decisions and, in general, do just about anything necessary to divorce a couple and settle all financial issues between married couples or affecting the welfare of children.

People tend to underestimate the authority of the Family Court, but it has a great deal of power and an international reach. Once the court obtains jurisdiction over a person (or a corporation or company) it has authority to order a wide range of relief. In *Bakala v. Bakala*, for example, the Family Court obtained jurisdiction over a Czech national

married to a South Carolinian and divided their property in Prague. Once the parties are within the jurisdiction of the Family Court, their property—regardless of where it is located—is also subject to the court's jurisdiction. The court can also join corporations, banks and businesses as parties and order them to pay marital funds or turn over property in their possession to the other party.

The Family Court is a specialized court. It only adjudicates family law issues, as well as certain juvenile criminal matters and abuse and neglect cases initiated by the Department of Social Services. There are currently over fifty Family Court judges in South Carolina, and they are elected for six-year terms by the General Assembly. They make all of the decisions in the Family Court. There are no jury trials in the Family Court. It is a "court of equity," in which one judge exercises enormous power over the lives of litigants, subject only to appeals to the Court of Appeals or the Supreme Court of South Carolina.

Marital litigation begins with the service of legal paperwork, a **summons** (a call to appear in court) and **complaint**, which sets out the identity of the parties, their residence, the jurisdiction of the court, the matter in controversy and the relief requested. These pleadings are filed with the clerk of court and are open to the public unless the record is sealed by an order of a Family Court judge. A family law case proceeds along the same lines and follows most of the same rules as a civil case, such as an automobile accident case. The spouse who commences the suit— **the plaintiff**—files the summons and complaint against **the defendant**—the other spouse—and may join any other party who is necessary to adjudicate the controversy—for example, where one spouse has deeded marital property to a third party (his or her parents or sibling) and the plaintiff wishes to have the court set aside the transaction and return the property to the marital estate. The defendant files an answer and usually a counterclaim setting out his or her claims against the plaintiff.

The rules of the Family Court require that the parties file a **financial declaration**. This is the **single most important document** in most divorce cases and indeed is a "road map" to the case.

The **financial declaration form**, which the Family Court insists all litigants complete accurately, swear to under oath and file with the court, usually is more important than any other document in marital litigation. [www.judicial.state.sc.us/forms] Anyone getting a divorce needs to devote as much time as necessary to producing an accurate financial declaration.

The Supreme Court has decreed that a Family Court case shall be disposed of within 365 days of its filing or the case will be stricken. Thus, lawyers and litigants must move the case ahead or dismiss it.

One of the chief differences between marital litigation and other litigation is that frequently there is a flurry of activity at the beginning of the case because the parties have been unable to resolve who is going to live in the house pending a final settlement, who is going to have temporary custody of the children, how much temporary support is going to be paid, what is going to happen to various properties, businesses and accounts and how debts are going to be paid. This is what lawyers call the **temporary phase** of the case, and it sometimes can be quite protracted and expensive. (Because lawyers still love Latin and pomposity, a temporary hearing is called a "*pendente lite*" hearing, or a hearing to determine what will happen while the litigation is pending.)

The phrase "legal separation" has no real meaning in South Carolina law. However, where the parties enter into a formal separation agreement or have a temporary order, they have, in effect a "legal separation." Of course, people can separate amicably with no agreement or order and their separation is still "legal." One does not have to "register" or "file" anything in order to be legally separated.

Temporary ("*Pendente Lite*") Relief

Where the parties are able to agree on who will have possession of the home, custody of the children, pay the debts and how the finances will be handled until a final settlement can be reached, there is no need for a temporary hearing. Many parties reach an agreement on temporary issues. Obviously, the wisest course is to reach such an agreement, if possible. But, "It takes two to tango." In many cases, the parties were fighting while they were married and they continue to disagree during the separation. Thus, where both parties want to remain in the home or both parties want custody of the children or the wife wants alimony but the husband does not want to pay it, the matter comes before the Family Court, sometimes on an emergency basis, in what is called a motion for temporary (*pendente lite)* relief.

Motions for temporary relief can be complicated, time-consuming and expensive for a variety of reasons. The most obvious is a custody case. Two people cannot have sole custody of a child. Where there is a real contest, both parties have the right to ask a judge to award him or her custody and the other party visitation. This can involve a great deal of work for the lawyers, who must obtain numerous affidavits of witnesses and other evidence. If there are allegations of physical or sexual abuse, one party will seek custody and no visitation or supervised visitation by the other spouse. These kinds of cases are the most complicated known to family law practitioners.

Temporary hearings, which lawyers often describe as "affidavit ambush," are governed by Rule 21 of the South Carolina Rules of Family Court, which provides as follows: "Evidence received by the court at temporary hearings shall be confined to pleadings, affidavits, and financial declarations unless good cause is shown to the court why additional evidence or testimony may be necessary."

This means literally that a party can be served with a summons, complaint and motion for temporary relief, and the temporary hearing can be held within five days of service. Unfortunately, the system is subject to abuse because one party could have been planning the divorce for months and drawn up ten affidavits from friends and family, financial experts and others, while the other party is not even aware that a divorce is about to take place. In the absence of a *bona fide* emergency, most judges will continue a motion for temporary relief to allow the defendant time to prepare. But, of course, a judge may not allow such time if he or she thinks it is a true emergency. Therefore, **if a party is served with a motion for temporary relief, he or she should immediately contact a lawyer and begin preparing a defense.**

There is no prescribed procedure for temporary hearings. Most judges allow lawyers to make brief arguments based on the affidavits and moving papers. Some judges restrict the lawyers to stating what relief they want for their client. The hearings are brief. Judges may rule from the bench or take the matter under advisement and rule later.

Motions for temporary relief almost always revolve around money, possession of the house or custody. "My husband," Roseanne Barr quipped, "said he needed more space, so I locked him outside." This is the kind of event that triggers a temporary hearing. People generally do not fight about which car they are going to drive during the pendency of the litigation or who is going to control a family business, although they could. Indeed, any issue can be contested at a temporary hearing. Judges sometimes must decide which school the children should go to on a temporary basis; who should have possession of the family pet; who should have possession of which bank accounts; who should pay which bills; and which party, if either, should advance money for legal fees to the other. All of these matters are discretionary with the judge. The word "discretion" is important because the appellate courts recognize that there are a myriad of problems, details, time constraints and practical issues that have to be resolved by a judge who may or may not have sufficient time to devote to resolving the matter. In the fifteen minutes generally allotted, no testimony is taken.

Yet sometimes a divorce case hinges on the temporary hearing. For example, the couple may be fighting over custody of children and who will live in the marital home. The person in the home usually gets custody of the children, and temporary hearings can determine both. The Family Court cannot order a spouse out of the house just because they are bickering. Getting the other spouse out of the house and keeping custody of the children is sometimes the biggest problem in a case. Judges will order a separation where there are fault grounds—adultery, physical cruelty or habitual drunkenness— but "incompatibility" or "mental cruelty" will not suffice. Sometimes the wronged spouse is forced to leave the house in order to get into Family Court, as Family Court judges are not in the business of settling domestic quarrels between spouses living together.

I have referred to the temporary hearing aspect of a family law case as "speedy injustice." Family Court judges attempt to do the right thing, and most of the time the decisions are very fair, or at least fair enough that the parties can live with them. Sometimes the temporary results are unfair because the lawyer for one party was not prepared or the judge misunderstood the facts or the law. But it is unrealistic to expect that any judge, no matter how patient, wise or fair, can regularly look at mounds of paper containing numerous and contradictory affidavits about everything ranging from the welfare of children to how much the parties earn and make totally well-informed, temporary decisions. The judges themselves frequently tell the litigants that a temporary order is the best the court can do under the circumstances, a temporary order is designed to preserve the *status quo* and everything will be reviewed carefully at a trial on the merits of the case. "When I hear of 'equity' in a case like this," Lord Bowen observed, "I am reminded of a blind man in a dark room—looking for a black hat—which isn't there." Temporary orders are generally (but not always) unappealable.

The temporary procedures in Family Court aim to preserve the *status quo*, allow both parties sufficient assets and income to live, ensure the safety and well-being of the children, provide access to the children by both parties and allow both parties to fairly litigate the case. Thus, where the wife is a stay-at-home mother or has a modest income and the husband has a much greater income, Family Court judges usually award temporary attorney's fees and costs to allow the wife to litigate the case and to have a "level playing field." Most attorneys will require some type of retainer for his or her fees before embarking on motions for temporary relief. Judges tend to believe that temporary hearings are just that—temporary. They believe that all they are doing, generally speaking, is preserving the *status quo*, resolving the parties' differences as equitably as they can given the limited resources and the lack of live testimony. Their intent is that the temporary order not prejudice either party and, in fact, it is customary to include in the temporary order that the order was based on affidavits and therefore should not be used as a precedent at the trial.

In truth, however, a temporary hearing can often determine the outcome of the case. First, some parties to the litigation have an unrealistic view of what is going to happen in Family Court. They believe they are going to win custody when they do not have a chance to do so; or that they are going to retain possession of the house, which they will not; or that they are entitled to more alimony and child support than the court realistically will grant them. They may have an inflated view of their spouse's income or assets or be totally in the dark about the financial realities of the marriage. Rather than see the temporary hearing as a way to temporarily resolve matters pending a trial, these litigants often become disheartened and more willing to settle because they believe the system has not treated them fairly and therefore will not in the future. Thus, a victory at the temporary hearing will sometimes give a party the opportunity to settle the case on favorable terms because the losing party loses heart, momentum or the will to fight.

Temporary hearings can also create problems for the victor. Many litigants achieve results at the temporary hearing out of proportion to what they actually will obtain at the final hearing. For example, I have been in cases where judges have awarded $18,000 per month in temporary alimony, a number that proved to be wholly inappropriate at the end of the case. Litigants who "win big" at temporary hearings can develop an unrealistic view about what can be accomplished when the case is tried on the merits.

The problem is particularly acute in custody cases, because whoever is granted temporary custody may then attempt to delay the trial for as long as possible so that he or she can have a track record showing what a great parent he or she is. The litigant who does not win feels demoralized and that it will be difficult to win a contested custody case. This creates enormous strain on the parties and the attorneys.

Custody litigation is expensive. Litigants are understandably emotionally distressed and feel that they need to spend whatever is necessary in order to protect their children. Lawyers view custody cases as the death penalty cases of Family Court. Consequently, some judges at temporary hearings now award joint custody or sometimes award each parent half of the time with the children or give the noncustodial parent much more visitation than they would at the trial on the merits. This then leads to the phenomenon just discussed, namely that if the noncustodial parent has more visitation than they would normally be entitled to in a final trial, it becomes more difficult to settle the case.

In short, temporary hearings can sometimes determine the outcome of the litigation even though the law holds that they are not binding and have no precedential value.

Where there is criminal domestic violence, the victim of domestic abuse has a plethora of rights under the Protection from Domestic Abuse Act, §20-4-10 to §20-4-160 S.C. Code. [www.judicial.state.sc.us] Any family member can, without a lawyer, file for protection from domestic abuse in Family Court. The court has the authority to issue an order of protection that restrains the abuse. The Family Court can also award temporary relief (custody, support, possession of the home, restraining orders as to property and attorney's fees) in these types of proceedings. The forms are also online at www.judicial. state.sc.us/forms.

Discovery

Once the parties have filed suit and resolved their temporary issues, the next stage in litigation is "discovery." **Discovery** consists of the lawyers sending to each other lists of questions, called **interrogatories**, designed to elicit from the other side the basic facts of the case (bank accounts, credit card accounts, life insurance information, etc.), the names of the witnesses and the party's position on various matters. Another part of discovery is the **request for production of documents**, which asks the opposing side for evidence, records and documents such as tax returns, cancelled checks, credit card records, e-mails, electronic information and financial statements. The process of discovery also involves the **request to admit**, in which one party asks the other party to admit facts, such as the fact that the opposing party has committed adultery or makes a certain amount of money. The party receiving the request to admit has to admit or deny the requests within thirty days or the allegations will be taken as true.

Yet another form of discovery involves **depositions**, which are useful, although they can be expensive. A deposition typically involves a lawyer subpoenaing witnesses to his or her office. These witnesses can then be asked questions under oath before a court reporter, just as if they were in court. A transcript of the testimony is prepared by the reporter. Judges take depositions seriously, because the party or the witness is under oath and giving testimony as if in court. And it is difficult for a witness to say one thing at a deposition and something else at the trial; judges frown on that. The cliché question lawyers always ask when a witness gives different testimony at the trial from the testimony he or she gave at a deposition is, "Were you lying under oath then or are you lying under oath now?"

Most people hate to be involved in lawsuits, dislike being witnesses and particularly dislike being involved in divorce or custody cases. Litigants are always surprised to learn that friends and neighbors who vociferously told them anything and everything they knew about the other spouse become mute and absolutely, positively do not want to be involved in their case, even though they have valuable evidence to give the court. One of the most frustrating tasks for lawyers is convincing witnesses such as neighbors, teachers, ministers, priests, psychologists and doctors to give affidavits at temporary hearings or to testify in court. Witnesses can be subpoenaed to come to a deposition or a trial, but if they do not want to be involved in the case, their testimony may not be exactly as the client envisioned it. This is particularly true of family members. Many naïve litigants believe that the other spouse's family members will tell the truth. They tend to be chagrined when they learn that "blood is thicker than water."

Usually, the discovery process goes smoothly. Rule 25 of the Rules of Family Court encourages "the prompt voluntary exchange of information." Lawyers can agree to exchange documents without sending official requests for production of documents or interrogatories. Accountants hired by both sides or a joint CPA can, oftentimes, pull together the necessary financial documents without the necessity of formal discovery. **Discovery is not mandatory so long as both parties feel they have had full financial disclosure and the lawyers and CPAs are comfortable they know all the facts.** Discovery is not limited to South Carolina. When one of the parties has a business or bank account in another state, the Family Court can issue a subpoena for records, which will be honored in other states. Many banks, credit card companies and other businesses now have "subpoena compliance centers" to handle requests for information.

On other occasions, discovery can be frustrating, particularly when one side decides to "stonewall" the other and not produce relevant documents. The lawyers then have to file motions to compel, which require the other party to fully answer interrogatories and to produce all the documents requested. This can be time-consuming and expensive. Some clients refuse to turn over documents or cooperate in disclosing assets. Judges can become frustrated with these motions because they involve a lot of detail. Judges are forced to go through each interrogatory and each document request to determine whether the questions have been answered and the documents produced.

Sometimes judges will award fees to the moving party if they feel the other party acted in bad faith by suppressing evidence. Other times, judges do not award fees even though the party seeking the documents has spent a great deal of time and money in order to get them.

Alternative Dispute Resolution

The next step in the process is mediation or some other alternative dispute resolution process, such as arbitration or collaborative law. The courts of South Carolina have virtually mandated mediation or arbitration in all contested cases. While the Supreme Court of South Carolina has issued orders mandating mediation in certain counties, the Family Court judges have the authority to require the parties to mediate and the judges almost always do. **Mediation is the most common alternative dispute resolution process.** It is completely voluntary. It is, in essence, a structured settlement conference with an impartial mediator or negotiator meeting with the parties (usually in

separate rooms), shuttling back and forth (sometimes all day) until a voluntary agreement can be reached. Arbitration is usually binding, although one can have nonbinding arbitration. Arbitration amounts to hiring a "private judge" to decide the issues. Collaborative law involves non-litigating lawyers and others, such as therapists and accountants, in non-adversarial settlement or negotiation sessions without a neutral third party.

All forms of alternative dispute resolution are good if the participants are knowledgeable and participate in good faith. Many divorce lawyers were initially opposed to mediation because they did not want inexperienced lawyers, social workers and others not familiar with divorce laws trying to convince people to settle when they had insufficient financial disclosure or the mediators were unfamiliar with the legal rights of the parties. This remains a problem because anyone can be a mediator, and if a mediator—no matter how well intentioned—does not understand the legal rights of the parties, if there is not full financial disclosure or if one party is bullying the other party, the mediation is unlikely to produce a fair resolution. Most mediators, however, are experienced Family Court lawyers who do understand what the parties' rights are and can help to settle most cases.

It is up to the lawyer, accountant and other experts to prepare the parties for mediation or arbitration by producing a comprehensive and accurate financial declaration. Lawyers and accountants also have a duty to come to the mediation with full financial disclosure, proper values for all assets (or at least acceptable estimates) and knowledge of the true income and expenses of the parties. Depending on the case, other information may be necessary in order to settle the case, such as health insurance, life insurance, credit card and other debts, taxes and private school tuition. **There is no point in mediating if you are not prepared, and it is the lawyer's job to ensure that.**

Some clients think that the mediator can do all the work and that lawyers or accountants are not necessary. This is dangerous thinking. Mediators, like judges, only know what they are told. If you appear at the mediation without a lawyer or with an unprepared lawyer; if you do not understand the financial issues; if you are not aware of all the marital assets and their value; if you do not know the true income of the opposing party; if you do not understand the principles of law applicable to the division of property, alimony and child support, then the mediation process may not produce a fair result.

The good news is that over 90 percent of all cases in Family Court are settled by the parties, the attorneys or through the mediation process. Few cases actually go to trial, as trials are expensive and people do not want their personal business spread on the public record.

But if mediation fails, the only alternative is to go to trial or enter into an agreement for binding arbitration. Arbitration is a form of dispute resolution in which the parties enter into an arbitration agreement to allow an arbitrator to decide their case, just as a judge would. The decision to arbitrate is voluntary. A court cannot order the parties to participate in binding arbitration. But once a party agrees to arbitration, he or she must accept the result. There is no appeal, except under extremely limited circumstances, such as fraud.

There are many advantages to arbitration. The parties can settle some issues and have the arbitrator decide others. They can limit what the arbitrator can do, i.e., award no less than "X" amount of alimony but no more than "Y." Arbitration is private and it can be done quickly. If parties have done something illegal, such as fail to pay income taxes or violated other laws, an arbitrator, unlike a judge, is under no duty to report these activities to the authorities. Arbitrations are quick, informal and much less expensive than trials.

Trials and Their Aftermath

If all else fails, the parties take their case to trial. Trials in the Family Court are much like non-jury trials in other courts. One judge hears witnesses and receives evidence from the plaintiff and then the defendant. Each party testifies to all the facts and issues in the case:

the history of the marriage, each parties' contribution and fault, facts and opinions about the children if custody or visitation is an issue, all financial issues (assets, income, debt, lifestyle during the marriage), special needs of the parties (health insurance, life insurance, need for more education), who should stay in the house, how to divide all the assets (businesses, real estate, pensions included), who broke up the marriage and why, attorney's fees and a myriad of other issues.

Trials, depending on the complexity of the issues in the case, can last one day or several weeks. Custody cases are lengthy because they involve so many witnesses—the parties, friends, relatives, neighbors, pediatricians, teachers, ministers and experts such as doctors, psychiatrists, psychologists and counselors—and so much emotion. Many trials include the testimony of expert witnesses—certified public accountants, real estate appraisers, business valuation experts and personal property appraisers, among others. If adultery is contested, the court typically hears from private investigators, neighbors, coworkers and even computer experts who can find deleted e-mails and websites.

After the trial, the attorneys typically prepare proposed orders for the judge, including proposed "findings of fact" and "conclusions of law," describing what the facts are and the ruling ought to be. These findings and conclusions in the form of a final order, once signed by a judge, are similar to a verdict by a jury. Until the final order and decree of divorce are issued, the parties remain under the temporary order, which could have been issued up to a year before.

Once the final order is issued, either party may ask the court to change the order by filing a motion to alter or amend order, frequently (erroneously) referred to as a motion to reconsider. Once again, the judge has thirty days to pass on this motion. If the court realizes that it has made an erroneous ruling, it can be corrected. If not, the motion is denied and the final order stands as written.

A party dissatisfied with a final order may appeal within thirty days of written notice of entry of the order or judgment. Appeals are lengthy procedures. Ambrose Bierce defined an appeal as follows: "In law, to put the dice into the box for another throw." The appellant must order a transcript of the trial from the court reporter, which is expensive. The appellant must create a record for the Court of Appeals, including copies of exhibits. Both parties must write legal briefs setting out the Family Court's errors of fact or law and wait for the Court of Appeals to review the record, hear the arguments of the attorneys and issue an opinion. A party dissatisfied with the opinion of the Court of Appeals may petition the Supreme Court of South Carolina. However, the Supreme Court rarely hears divorce cases, but will do so where important issues of public policy are involved.

In truth, the Family Court system in South Carolina works well. It is, compared to many other states, relatively quick and accessible. But divorce is a messy, emotional process and the wisest judge and the smartest lawyer cannot undo the damage done by the divorce itself. **I see the Family Court system as a series of emergency rooms where lawyers and judges, like doctors and health care professionals, do the best they can with messy facts and emotionally charged patients.** Sometimes the result is excellent. At other times, the parties can just walk away happy to get out of the system. Unfortunately, for some, the results are tragic.

Chapter 2

Divorce

Judge: You want a divorce on the grounds that your husband is careless about his appearance?
Wife: Yes, your honor—he hasn't made one in three years.

More husbands would leave home if they knew how to pack their suitcase.

—Leopold Fetchner

Despite South Carolina's conservative history and tradition (it was the last state to allow divorce), the state's divorce laws are now in line with other states, although the state is still among the more conservative jurisdictions in domestic matters. South Carolina was late in adopting "no fault" divorce, which allowed for a divorce when the parties had lived separate and apart for a period of time, but did so in 1969, allowing divorce after a three-year separation. In 1979, the period of separation was amended to one year. South Carolina recognizes only one form of divorce, namely divorce *a vinculo matrimonii*: divorce from the bonds of matrimony.

Needless to say, in order to be divorced, one must be married. While it is unusual for parties who think they are married to learn they are not, it does happen. For example, a woman may have been married in her reckless teenage years and never bothered to divorce her first husband. She marries again, settles down, has two children and lives a respectable life. Twenty-five years later, in the midst of a divorce, her husband learns of the first marriage. If husband number one is still alive, technically there was no second marriage, because in order to marry one must have the capacity to marry, and one cannot marry if one is already married. The second marriage is not a common-law marriage, because in order for a relationship to ripen into a common-law marriage the parties must have the capacity to marry.

Similarly, some marriages are void or voidable because the spouses are too closely related by blood (consanguinity). In South Carolina, while first cousins may marry, a man cannot marry his niece, aunt or stepmother, among others. A marriage to a spouse younger than sixteen years of age is also void.

South Carolina is one of thirteen states that recognize common-law marriage—that is, a marriage without the benefit of a marriage license and a ceremony. Assuming each spouse is competent to marry, a man and a woman living together as husband and wife with the intent to be married and holding themselves out to the public as married have a common-law marriage, which is legally the same as any other marriage. They need not live together for any specific period. Many

people believe the couple must live together for seven years, but this is a myth. The intent to be married, however, must be proven. Evidence typically includes living together as a married couple, publicly telling people they are married, filing joint tax returns and the use of the man's name by the woman.

Most people who are divorced in South Carolina are divorced on the ground of one year's separation with no fault. **All that is necessary to obtain a divorce in South Carolina is to prove that one is a bona fide resident, that one is married, that the parties have resided separate and apart for more than one year without cohabitation, that there is no collusion between the parties and that there is no possibility of a reconciliation.** One must be a resident of South Carolina to obtain a divorce. If both parties reside in South Carolina, the length of required residency is three months. If only one party resides in South Carolina, then it is one year. You can be divorced in South Carolina even if your spouse lives in another state, but South Carolina would not have authority to award support or divide property unless you last lived together as husband and wife in South Carolina or your spouse agreed to the jurisdiction of the South Carolina courts.

The "collusion" and "reconciliation" requirements are remnants of a bygone era when the courts were concerned that the parties colluded or conspired to create grounds for divorce (such as adultery) that in fact did not exist in order to obtain a divorce, which was frowned upon by state policy and societal attitudes. Testimony that there was no collusion between the parties is perfunctory.

It must also be said that efforts at reconciliation made by the court are normally futile. The judge questions the parties to determine if there is any possibility of reconciliation, and may ask them whether counseling would help. **Although an attempt to reconcile may be perfunctory, it is a reversible error for a judge not to do it!** So long as one party testifies that reconciliation is not possible, even though the other party believes it is, the court will grant the divorce. I was in one explosive case in which the parties' hatred for

each other knew no bounds, and when the judge asked if there was any possibility of reconciliation, everyone in the courtroom, including the judge, laughed out loud.

Thus, if one party is determined to obtain a divorce, the court will grant it, provided the parties have been separated for more than one year. **Separated means separated.** Living in separate bedrooms in the same house is not living separate and apart. A separation caused by military service is also not separation.

There are people who simply do not want to be divorced; some for religious or moral reasons, others for psychological or emotional reasons, a few to retain their health insurance. But there is no way to prevent a divorce from taking place. The fact that a client refuses to "cooperate" in obtaining a divorce is meaningless, because one party can serve a summons and complaint asking for a divorce, serve it on the other party and demand a hearing. Even if the defendant flees the state and disappears, he or she can be served by publication of the pleadings in the newspaper. Therefore, if the wife wants to obtain a divorce on the ground of adultery or physical cruelty, the husband cannot prevent her from doing it by any means short of negotiating the grounds for divorce in the overall settlement. While technically one cannot enter into an enforceable contract to obtain a divorce, the parties and the lawyers can reach a workable understanding.

The old remark that "my wife refuses to give me a divorce" is left over from another time in history. **Neither party can prevent the other party from obtaining a divorce on any ground that they legitimately have.**

In addition to living separate and apart for one year, there are other grounds for divorce, namely the traditional fault grounds of adultery, physical cruelty, habitual drunkenness or addiction to drugs and desertion for a period of one year. One cannot be divorced in South Carolina for "incompatibility" or "mental cruelty." As G.K. Chesterton observed, "I believe it is possible to obtain a divorce in the United States on the grounds of incompatibility. If that is true, I am surprised there are any marriages left in the United States."

The fault grounds each have a long history, and each requires proof by a preponderance of the evidence and in some cases, namely adultery, by "clear and convincing evidence." There are legal, moral, religious, strategic, psychological and financial reasons to pursue or not to pursue fault grounds. As will be made abundantly clear throughout this book, fault is a significant factor and sometimes a major factor in divorce cases in South Carolina. When one spouse commits adultery, physically abuses the other or is an alcoholic or drug addict, fault can play a significant role in the award of support, property division, custody, child support, legal fees and every other issue in the case.

It is not necessary to sue for divorce on a fault ground to prove fault in one's case for custody, alimony or property division. The wronged spouse can prove adultery, physical cruelty, desertion or habitual drunkenness in order to convince the court to award more alimony, property or custody of children and still not actually file for divorce. Fault is a factor in all of the foregoing, with or without a divorce action.

Adultery is a common cause of divorce, and the innocent spouse frequently wishes to prove adultery as a ground for divorce. Proof of adultery must be "clear and positive" and established by "a clear preponderance of the evidence." In *DuBose v. DuBose*, the Supreme Court held that although proof of adultery must be sufficiently definite as to time, place and circumstances, insufficiency of proof would not defeat a divorce where the judge believed adultery had occurred. In that case, the paramour denied having sexual relations with the wife. He did, however, make a few damaging admissions. When asked if he had committed adultery with the wife he said, "I think it would be mighty sorry man that would, don't you?"

In *Prevatte v. Prevatte*, Mr. Prevatte was discovered parking at night in a remote location, a graveyard, with a woman other than his wife.

Judge Sanders observed:

> If it were not for the circumstantial evidence, the practice of adultery would not scarcely be known to exist...For example, where a married man is observed going upstairs in a bawdyhouse, unless something to the contrary appears, no other evidence is required to warrant a finding of adultery. The opportunities available to Mr. Prevatte are quite apparent... When two people, a man and a woman, park by themselves at night in lonely places and purposely sit very close together, unless some other reason appears for their behavior, even the most dispassionate observer may very well infer that they are romantically disposed toward each other. Such is life...The trial judge, not having been born yesterday, was convinced that Mr. Prevatte had committed adultery. So are we.

Adultery traditionally was defined as the voluntary sexual intercourse of a married person with someone of the opposite sex other than the offender's spouse. This simple formula is no longer the law. In *Doe v. Doe*, the question arose as to whether an act of fellatio was an act of adultery. The wife admitted that she engaged in a single act of fellatio. The South Carolina Code does not define the term adultery. Judge Sanders opined, "Definitions of fellatio are available from a number of sources, but not this opinion," and that the "paucity of legal precedent on the issue whether fellatio is adultery suggests that it is not one which society cries out to have resolved." Because the husband had condoned whatever sexual acts the wife had performed, the court evaded the issue. Homosexual sex is adultery.

Because adultery must be proven by clear and convincing evidence, many litigants need the service of a private investigator. **Because judges are loath to make a finding of adultery if there is room to doubt, it is wise to get the best proof available before accusing the other spouse.** As Milton Berle observed, "A caring husband is a man so interested in his wife's happiness that he will hire a detective to find out who is responsible for it."

Physical cruelty has been defined as "actual personal violence, or such a course of physical treatment as endangers life, limb or health, and renders cohabitation unsafe." Judges look at the circumstances of each particular case. Continued acts of personal violence producing physical pain or bodily injury and a fear of future danger is sufficient cause for a divorce on the grounds of physical cruelty, especially when accompanied by other acts of ill treatment. Slight violence or threats are not sufficient. Ordinarily, a single act of physical cruelty will not constitute grounds for divorce, but such an act accompanied by an intention to do serious bodily harm or that causes reasonable apprehension of serious danger in the future would suffice. Of course, if the person guilty of physical cruelty was sufficiently provoked to do it, there can be no divorce on physical cruelty.

In *McKenzie v. McKenzie*, Mrs. McKenzie was found to have "unjustifiably" shot at Mr. McKenzie four times "from close range." Mr. McKenzie, understandably, was seriously wounded and therefore was entitled to a divorce on the ground of physical cruelty. In *Gill v. Gill*, Mrs. Gill caught Mr. Gill at a motel with his girlfriend. She shot him with a pellet gun. She also allegedly rammed his car with her car, or possibly Mr. Gill put on his brakes to cause the accident. But Mr. Gill was not entitled to a divorce on the ground of physical cruelty because, apparently, he was not actually afraid of Mrs. Gill!

As George Coote said, "No woman has ever shot her husband while he was doing the dishes."

Desertion for a period of one year, once the most common ground for divorce, has now been abandoned for other grounds. Why bother

alleging desertion for a year when one can obtain a no-fault divorce on one year's separation? Nevertheless, one can still obtain a divorce on the fault ground of desertion if one can prove cessation of cohabitation for a year, the intent not to return, absence of consent and the absence of a just reason for the deserting spouse to leave. The parties must have lived separate and apart for one year. A deserting spouse may defeat the divorce by a good faith offer to return. If the deserted spouse refuses to allow the deserting spouse to return, the original deserter may claim the original deserted is the deserter. But when one spouse is solely responsible for marital discord and the other spouse was justified in leaving, that spouse cannot sue on the ground of desertion.

Habitual drunkenness has also been a traditional ground for divorce. Given the prevalence of drug addiction in our society, the ground now includes "habitual drunkenness caused by the use of narcotic drug." (Apparently some drug use, such as habitually smoking marijuana, is not sufficient, as marijuana is not a narcotic drug.) "Habitual drunkenness" has not been defined by the courts, but alcoholism is clearly grounds for divorce if it is a "fixed habit" of drinking and causes the breakdown of the marriage. The condition must, however, exist at or near the time of the filing of the action for divorce. One cannot divorce a reformed alcoholic on the ground of habitual drunkenness. To obtain a divorce on account of addiction to drugs, the drug abuser must be dependent on drugs or be a habitual user.

Many people wonder if their marriage can be annulled. The answer is almost always "No," because an annulment means you were never legally married, which is quite unusual. Annulments are proper when one spouse finds out that the other spouse is married to someone else still living. This type of marriage was not legal, because one spouse did not have the capacity to marry. Other examples are marriages between family members, which are forbidden by law, or where the marriage is never consummated. Fraud can also vitiate a marriage if one spouse lied about something critical to the marriage, such as impotency, or one is forced to marry at gunpoint. But the courts are wary of annulling "shotgun weddings" (a case of wife or death) because of the implications for the children involved. Eddie Albert once quipped, "I wanted to marry her ever since I saw the moonlight shining on the barrel of her father's shotgun." (There is a real South Carolina "shotgun wedding" case on the books. In *Phipps v. Phipps*, Mr. Phipps got Mrs. Phipps pregnant and her father and brother threatened to shoot Mr. Phipps if he did not marry his future bride).

A divorce can only be granted on grounds allowed by South Carolina law. A man cannot divorce a wife for refusing to have sex with him—Rhett Butler's threat to Scarlett ("You know I can divorce you for this!") notwithstanding. Even scandalous or abusive behavior, or publicly subjecting the wife to indignities (In *Levin v. Levin*, Mr. Levin wrongfully charged his wife with adultery in her father's home and insisted on sexual relations "when his wife's physical condition made his doing so indecent") are not grounds for divorce. A nagging wife can nag away and not be divorced for it. "Unpleasantness of the wife is a risk assumed by the husband," our court has held, in *Brown v. Brown*! Insanity is not a ground for divorce. Death terminates the marriage without divorce, although a claim for property division survives the death of a spouse, if marital litigation is pending.

The law encourages reconciliation. Thus, when an erring spouse is forgiven by the other spouse, the divorce grounds disappear. When a wife forgives an adulterous husband and they reconcile, she no longer has grounds for divorce—unless he does it again. Forgiveness is called condonation, and it is a defense to a divorce. "It operates," the Court of Appeals held in 1859, "as an amnesty in regard to all prior grievances."[1]

The law, in its infinite wisdom, denies a divorce to two erring spouses. Thus, where both husband and wife commit adultery and one does not want the divorce, he or she can raise the defense of "recrimination." Two sinners, it seems, must remain married to each other. (Recrimination does not, however, prevent a divorce on one year's separation.)

Finally, the state jealously guards its right to grant or withhold divorces. A contract to obtain a divorce is void as against public policy. Where the parties agreed in a separation agreement that they could "date" who they wanted, this did not mean that the innocent party consented to adultery on the part of the other party. The parties cannot agree on grounds for divorce—at least not in a legally enforceable agreement. One spouse may agree to forgo obtaining a divorce against the other for adultery, but he or she cannot be held to such an agreement in court.

Chapter 3

Alimony

Alimony—the cash surrender value of a husband.

I'll never marry again. I've got your alimony to keep me warm.
> —Nancy Kelly (Valerie) to divorced husband Joel
> McCrea (T.H. Randall) in *He Married His Wife*
> (20ᵗʰ Century Fox, 1940)

If, as we shall see, a contested custody case is the death penalty trial of Family Court, a contested alimony case is seen by many husbands as mandatory life imprisonment—with the possibility of parole. Forty years ago, lawyers and judges assumed a wife was entitled to alimony (spousal support) where the husband earned more than she did, which was typically the case, and where the wife had not committed adultery. It is not the law that has undergone significant changes, but rather our society.

Today it is not uncommon for husbands and wives to earn equivalent salaries. Indeed, it is not uncommon for wives to earn more than husbands. Thus, women or dependent husbands have the ability or potential ability to support themselves and, therefore, do not need support from their spouses. Many modern women resent the idea of being financially dependent on their husbands.

But the law in South Carolina has not deviated from its essential features over the centuries: the dependent spouse, usually the wife, is entitled to support where

- There are grounds for divorce or for "separate maintenance and support," i.e., the parties are living apart
- One of the parties needs alimony to live a reasonable lifestyle
- The needy spouse is truly dependent, unable to work or earns far less than the other spouse
- There is a significant disparity in income
- There is usually a marriage of some length, i.e., not a short marriage
- There are young children in the care of the wife
- The other spouse has the ability to pay

A dependent spouse (or "payee") is entitled to temporary alimony while the case is being litigated, provided he or she has made a *prima facie* showing of probable cause for divorce or separation. Alimony must be determined in the divorce litigation, or the spouse's right to it is forever lost (unless the court explicitly preserves the issue). Once the issue of spousal support has been litigated in a separation proceeding and it has been denied, alimony may not be raised in the subsequent divorce proceeding unless the court reserves jurisdiction over the issue in the separation decree.

Alimony is governed by a statute found at §20-3-130 through §20-7-170 of the South Carolina Code of Laws (www.sccourts.org, www.scstatehouse.net or www.straighttalkscdivorce.com). This law

describes what alimony is, what the powers of the Family Court are to award it, the factors to be considered and how it might be secured.

Six Types of Alimony

There are six types of alimony under South Carolina law:

1. Permanent, Periodic Alimony

This is the traditional type of alimony comedians joke about and husbands, and now some wives (whoever is the "payor"), fear. As in, "Alimony is always having to say you're sorry" (Philip J. Simborg) and, "Alimony is like buying oats for a dead horse" (Arthur Baer).

The jokes notwithstanding, **the law of South Carolina favors permanent, periodic alimony over all other forms of spousal support.** The reason is simple: a spouse owes a duty of support to the other spouse (provided he or she can afford to pay) based on their lifestyle during the marriage. If the payor spouse dies, the alimony ends, as would his or her support of the other spouse had the payor died while they were married. If the payee spouse remarries or becomes self-supporting, alimony terminates. All other forms of alimony require a special showing of specific circumstances. **Periodic alimony terminates on the remarriage of the payee or death of either spouse,** unless the court provides that the alimony is secured by a life insurance policy insuring the life of the payor. Periodic alimony can be modified by the court where there is a material or substantial change in the circumstances of the parties. It is usually deductible to the payor for federal and state income tax and taxable to the payee.

2. Lump Sum Alimony

The law long ago recognized that in some rare instances, permanent, periodic alimony would not work. For example, where a husband had fled the jurisdiction or was unlikely to obey a court order, a lump sum or definite amount of alimony could be ordered. The husband's property could be seized to satisfy his duty of support.

Lump sum alimony may be paid in one installment or periodically over a period of time. It is distinguishable from periodic alimony in that it is for a finite sum. Thus, the payor knows exactly what he or she must pay (for example, $2,000 a month for five years, or $120,000). This type of alimony is ordinarily not terminable or modifiable based upon remarriage or a future change in circumstances. Lump sum alimony is generally terminable on the death of the payee, but need not be. **Lump sum alimony must be specifically requested.**

In the absence of an agreement between the parties, the court will not award lump sum alimony unless special circumstances require it or make it advisable. In *Hendricks v. Hendricks*, the court considered three factors in allowing a judge to order lump sum alimony: the husband's history of failure to provide support for his family, the husband's previous dissipation of large sums of money and the wife's current need for a lump sum payment. In *Jones v. Jones*, the husband's excessive use of alcohol and his unwillingness to support his family supported a lump sum alimony award. Desertion, remarriage and relocation to another state can also justify lump sum alimony.

3. Rehabilitative Alimony

The purpose of rehabilitative alimony is to encourage the payee spouse to become self-supporting by providing alimony for a limited period of time, during which the payee may be retrained and rehabilitated. **The benefit of this form of alimony is that it limits the time in which the payor spouse is burdened by alimony and permits the parties to develop their own independent lives.** If, however, the dependent spouse has been out of the job market and performing spousal duties over the course of a lengthy marriage, permanent, periodic alimony, rather than rehabilitative alimony, is appropriate. The Court of Appeals has frequently reversed the trial court where full rehabilitation cannot genuinely be achieved. There must be clear evidence demonstrating the payee spouse's self-sufficiency at the expiration of the ordered payments.

The court must make specific findings to support rehabilitative alimony. In practice, the payor spouse must demonstrate the time necessary for the payee spouse to acquire job skills, the likelihood he or she will successfully complete retraining and the likelihood of  his or her success in the job market. The level of self-sufficiency is based upon the standard of living the spouse enjoyed during the marriage. Thus, the payee's income after rehabilitation must at least approach the income of the payor during the marriage. In practice, this can rarely be accomplished. The payee's age is significant. The cutoff for rehabilitative alimony appears to be somewhere around the mid-forties.

Rehabilitative alimony may be paid in one installment or periodically. It is terminable upon the remarriage of the payee, the death of either spouse or when the payee becomes employed. An award can be secured by a life insurance policy on the payor's life. Rehabilitative alimony is also modifiable upon a showing of unforeseen events that either frustrate the good faith efforts of the payee to become self-supporting or affect the ability of the payor to pay.

4. Reimbursement Alimony

Reimbursement alimony may be ordered when the court determines it is necessary and desirable to reimburse one spouse from the other spouse's future earnings. **Reimbursement alimony may be appropriate when one spouse has supported the other while he or she obtained a license or an advanced degree.** For example, in *Donahue v. Donahue*, the wife supported her husband and put him through dental school. He left her for another woman after obtaining his degree and opening his practice, but before he began earning a substantial income. There was just something wrong with that picture, or as the court said, "an unfairness has occurred that calls for a remedy."

Cases like this may also justify a larger distribution of the marital assets to the working wife. However, a larger percentage of the marital assets may not be sufficient when little or no marital property has been accumulated. (Professional degrees, such as a medical degree, are not marital property subject to division.) Likewise, an award of periodic or lump sum alimony may not provide an adequate remedy.

Our courts have adopted a broad approach to reimbursement alimony. The courts will consider the amount of the wife's contribution, the wife's foregone opportunities to enhance or improve her professional or vocational skills, the duration of the marriage following the completion of the husband's professional education and the money expended for the support of the parties' children and the children from a previous marriage. Reimbursement alimony may be paid in a single or periodic installments. It is terminable on the wife's remarriage or upon the death of either spouse, unless the order provides for life insurance. It is not terminable or modifiable upon a change in circumstance in the future.

5. Separate Maintenance and Support

Separate maintenance and support is for the support of a spouse while the marriage relationship continues. It is awarded based on the same factors and considerations as alimony, but the parties do not divorce for some reason.

6. Other Forms of Alimony

The Family Court may also award "such other forms of spousal support, under such terms and conditions as the court may consider just, as appropriate under the circumstances without limitation to grant more than one form of support." The alimony statute allows the court to be creative with alimony. Judges have the flexibility to create a special form of alimony where equity requires. Thus, for example, a wife or husband could be entitled to permanent, periodic alimony and rehabilitative alimony for the specific purpose of funding his or her education for a better paying job.

Alimony Factors

The factors that judges use to determine alimony, i.e., the guidelines that the Family Court (and therefore lawyers, mediators and arbitrators) must take into account in setting an amount of alimony, are:

- the duration of the marriage and the ages of the parties at the time of the marriage and at the time of the divorce;
- the physical and emotional condition of each spouse;
- the educational background of each spouse, together with the need of each spouse for additional training or education;
- the employment history and earning potential of each spouse;
- the standard of living established during the marriage;
- the current and reasonably anticipated earnings of both spouses;
- the current and reasonably anticipated expenses and needs of both spouses;
- the marital and nonmarital properties of the parties, including those apportioned in the divorce;
- custody of the children, particularly where conditions or circumstances render it appropriate that the custodian not be required to seek employment outside the home, or where the employment must be of a limited nature;
- marital misconduct or fault of either or both parties, if the misconduct affects or has affected the economic circumstances of the parties, or contributed to the breakup of the marriage;
- the tax consequences to each party as a result of the particular form of support awarded;
- the existence and extent of any support obligation from a prior marriage or for any other reason of either party;
- such other factors the court considers relevant.

The most important factors by far are need and ability to pay. While alimony is not exactly welfare, and a long-suffering, model wife of forty years who has been wronged by a wayward husband should hardly be viewed as a welfare recipient, there are unspoken similarities. "Does the wife need alimony?" is the main question judges and lawyers ask. Why is she in need? Is she able to work and support herself? Will she receive sufficient assets to support herself? Does she have significant nonmarital funds? Can the husband afford to pay alimony without destroying his lifestyle and breeding such resentment that the parties will be in endless litigation? These are the chief practical considerations in evaluating an alimony claim.

Thus, where the forty-year-old schoolteacher earning $50,000 and the forty-five-year-old accountant earning $60,000 divorce, there will normally be no award of alimony. Where the doctor earning $300,000 runs off with the nurse and leaves behind the unemployed housewife or a teacher or clerk earning $25,000, the Family Court will undoubtedly order permanent, periodic alimony.

Age, health and the length of the marriage are major considerations. The divorce of a young couple in a short marriage would normally end with no provision for alimony. But the chances of alimony in a divorce involving an older couple in a long marriage are much greater.

Nevertheless, the results almost always come back to need. In *O'Neill v. O'Neill*, the parties had only been married nine years. Mrs. O'Neil had been married before and gave up alimony from her first husband. (Alimony terminates upon remarriage.) Mr. O'Neil had the ability to pay. The Family Court awarded Mrs. O'Neil $1,200 per month, where the husband testified he could earn $50,000 per year.

Fault is also a significant factor in alimony cases, and a wild card at that. "The wages of sin," Carolyn Wells said, "is alimony." The law as announced in the lawbooks is not always the law as announced in the courtroom. Here is where the subjectivity and values of individual judges are seen most clearly. The law in the books reminds one of contradictory clichés, such as "Hesitate and you are lost" versus

"Look before you leap." The cases hold, "Alimony is not intended to be a penalty for one spouse nor a reward for the other." However, "fault is a factor."[1]

Like contradictory clichés, the law ends up meaning different things to different people. If fault is indeed a factor that should be considered, then logically it, in the traditional case, is a reward to the wife and a punishment to the husband, which, in fact, is a consideration in actual practice, depending once again on how a particular judge views a particular set of facts. Much as one jury may award a deserving plaintiff $1 million for her pain and suffering and another jury award nothing, a Family Court judge is the finder of facts, using his or her discretion subject to the law, and the supervision of the Court of Appeals and the Supreme Court. Fault has been one of the most important factors in determining whether a party is entitled to support, and it will continue to be a significant consideration.

Fault as an Important Factor

Fault must be considered whether or not it is used as a basis for the divorce or separate maintenance action if the misconduct affects or has affected the economic circumstances of the parties or contributed to the breakup of the marriage. There is a limit, however. The misconduct must have occurred prior to the signing of a written property settlement agreement or the entry of a permanent order of separate maintenance and support or an order approving a property settlement agreement between the parties.

The most severe sanction for misconduct is the absolute bar of alimony for an adulterous spouse. Where either spouse commits adultery, he or she is barred from alimony. This is a harsh rule. A model wife of thirty years who has a brief affair at the end of the marriage when the parties are separated, even if her husband is an abusive, alcoholic, well-known philanderer and is also guilty of adultery, loses her alimony. And in spite of the harshness of the bar to alimony for adulterous spouses, the court may not compensate adulterous spouses by increasing their award of marital property. There have been efforts to change this statute in the General Assembly, but these efforts have failed to date.[2]

Homosexual activity between persons constitutes adultery for purposes of granting a divorce or barring alimony. Where the wife claims mental impairment as a defense to a divorce on the ground of adultery and the resulting bar to alimony, she must show that at the time she committed adultery, she was unable to appreciate the wrongfulness of the conduct.

Misconduct, other than adultery, may also justify the denial of alimony. Where the court finds that the disintegration of marriage was the fault of the wife, she could be denied alimony. This may be true even when the party seeking alimony is economically disadvantaged due to poor health. In one case, despite the husband's ill health and resulting economic disadvantage, the court held that his gross misconduct throughout the marriage justified denial of alimony. Habitual drunkenness will generally not bar alimony.

A court may, in its discretion, deny a wife alimony if she is egregiously at fault or guilty of indignities against the husband. Abandonment of the husband by the wife is not a bar to alimony, but may be considered as a fault factor.

Substantial fault can subject a husband to permanent alimony even after a short marriage. In *Johnson v. Johnson*, Dr. Johnson, a dentist, married a dental hygienist. He moved her from Columbia to his home in Greenwood, where he proceeded to severely mistreat her, mentally and physically. He battered her and hit her in the face. Citing *O'Neill*, the Court of Appeals held that, "If a claim for alimony is well-founded, the law favors the award of permanent, periodic alimony." Dr. Johnson claimed it was a short marriage of a little over one year, but Judge Bell held that Dr. Johnson "overlooks the fact that his own conduct was responsible for its quick demise" and that Mrs. Johnson was entirely blameless.

In a 2006 case, *Pirri v. Pirri*, the parties lived together without benefit of marriage for twenty-five years. The court found a common-law marriage beginning in 1996. Because it was, therefore, a short marriage, the Family Court denied Mrs. Pirri alimony. The Court of Appeals reversed and awarded Mrs. Pirri permanent alimony. The marriage may have been short, Judge Beatty correctly held, but the wife was sixty-seven and the husband was seventy-five. The short length of the marriage was *one* factor, but not the *only* factor.

Running the Numbers

In higher-income reported cases, the numbers run like this: In *Mallet v Mallet*, Mr. Mallet earned $441,191 annually. The parties were married for twenty-one years. Mrs. Mallet was a homemaker with a child at home. Mr. Mallet committed adultery. The Family Court awarded Mrs. Mallet $4,500 per month in support—which was, as alimony usually is, deductible to the husband for tax purposes and taxable to the wife—and $2,000 per month in (tax-free) child support. She also received 50 percent of the marital estate, which included her home. The Court of Appeals increased the alimony to $6,300 per month. The court gave the wife exactly what her financial declaration showed she needed: $8,300 per month for her and one child.

In *McElveen v. McElveen*, the Court of Appeals held that the trial court's award of $11,000 per month in alimony was excessive. Where the award eclipsed the largest alimony award of $6,300 (in *Mallet*) by $4,700, the parties lived affluent lifestyles and the husband made a substantial income; the wife's living expenses, as set forth in her financial declaration, were inflated; the wife did not present medical evidence indicating an inability to work; the wife sought to stay home due to the age of the child and not solely because of her alleged medical condition; and the award would deter the wife from seeking to improve her financial circumstances. The Court of Appeals reduced the alimony to $7,500 per month. Dr. McElveen earned $500,000 per year.

In more middle-class cases, the courts have done the following. In *Craig v. Craig*, Dr. Craig made $200,000 per year and was ordered to pay $3,000 per month in alimony. Mr. Jenkins paid Mrs. Jenkins $1,800 per month. Mr. Hickory was ordered to pay Mrs. Hickory $475 per month, where she earned $1,492 per month and he earned $3,255 per month. Mr. Deidun was required to pay Mrs. Dcidun $1,200 per month, where she earned $2,300 per month and he earned nearly $82,000 per year.

As we have seen (and contrary to popular belief), permanent, periodic alimony is *presumed* in South Carolina where there is a dependent spouse, except in marriages of short duration, the dependent spouse's adultery or other grievous fault on the part of that spouse.

National handbooks on divorce, like *Divorce for Dummies*, repeatedly say that permanent alimony "has pretty much gone the way of the typewriter, the eight-track tapes, and rotary phone," but these books **fail to accurately describe the law in South Carolina.**

If, in the traditional case, the wife commits adultery and the couple reconciles and the husband knows about her adultery, the slate is wiped clean, and she may be awarded alimony if they later divorce. This is known as condonation. It is a valid defense to the bar on alimony. "Recrimination" (both parties commit adultery), however, is not. The violation of the law by one's spouse does not justify or give license to the other to violate the same law without penalty.

Trying to kill your spouse may or may not bar alimony. In *Sharpe v. Sharpe*, the South Carolina Court of Appeals rejected a husband's contention that his wife should be barred from alimony because she confessed that she conspired to kill him. (Mrs. Sharpe was in prison. Therefore, the state may have had to provide her health care if the husband's health insurance did not.)

An award of alimony by a judge is discretionary. Payor spouses have the opportunity to argue that there was fault on the part of both parties, that the payee can support himself or herself and/or that the payor is willing for the payee to have a greater share of the assets (a paid-for house, a greater percentage of the retirement plan, more liquid assets) instead of alimony. A payor spouse's future earnings are sometimes the most valuable asset of the marriage. I have settled a case where the husband gave the wife 100 percent of the marital assets on the condition that she agreed to waive alimony. The husband kept all of his valuable future earnings.

The spouse seeking to minimize his or her alimony liability should moderate the parties' lifestyle and expenses; encourage his or her spouse to go to work if she or he is not working; pay his or her educational expenses or expenses of training or retraining him or her for a job; allow him or her to stay in the home if it is cost-effective or the mortgage is low or paid off; and provide an economic framework where the other spouse can be self-supporting.

Some wives, particularly older women, resent (understandably in my opinion) the notion that because the husband has run off with a younger woman, they must go back to work after being a homemaker for twenty years, raising the children and upholding their end of the marital bargain. These cases are emotional and contentious. The law, however, does require a wife—even if she has been mistreated—to contribute to her own support to the best of her ability. The Court of Appeals has held time and again that "alimony should not serve…as a disincentive for spouses to improve their employment potential or to dissuade them from providing, to the extent possible, for their own support." When a wife simply refuses to go to work, the husband's lawyer's job is to prove to the court that she can work by producing expert testimony from a vocational expert or by other means.

A typical plan for older spouses that is beneficial to both parties is for the dependent spouse to receive as many liquid assets (stocks, bonds, money market accounts, income-producing properties) as possible so that he or she can be self-supporting with his or her own assets. This provides security for the payee and decreases the payor's alimony obligation. A smaller house or condominium that has no mortgage benefits both parties: security for one, less alimony for the other.

Tax Planning

Tax advice and planning are essential to an alimony settlement. Because alimony is deductible, the state and federal governments actually contribute to the support of an ex-spouse. For example, in the traditional case, if the husband earns $200,000 per year, wife is unemployed and husband pays wife $5,000 per month in alimony, the wife will receive $3,943 per month after paying income tax and the husband will receive $7,692 per month. While the husband is paying $5,000 per month to the wife, it is actually costing him only $3,173 per month. Where the husband earns $150,000 and the wife earns $30,000, the husband pays $2,000 per month, the wife receives $1,436 per month in after-tax dollars and the husband's alimony costs him $1,339 per month.[3]

Taxes, of course, play a major role in all financial planning, which is why a competent accountant or financial advisor is a necessity in many divorce cases. Were the wife to receive $200,000 in municipal bonds, for example, she could earn 5 percent tax free and receive $10,000 per year, or $833 per month, tax free. If she receives a money market account of $200,000 and earns 5 percent, she would receive $10,000 per year, or $767per month, after paying taxes. Capital gains taxes must also be considered, because if a wife sells stock or liquidates a money market account, she may pay significant capital gains taxes. Clearly, both parties and their lawyers must investigate all of these issues carefully so that a fair result is reached.

Permanent, periodic alimony continues until the payee dies, remarries or cohabitates with another; the payor dies; or there is a material or substantial change of circumstance. Typical changes in circumstance arise from the payor's retirement or being terminated from his or her job, the payee's increased earnings or inheriting funds, the payor's decreased earnings or either party becoming disabled.

A spouse who receives alimony can no longer live with a person with whom he or she is romantically involved without benefit of marriage for longer than ninety days. S.C. Code Ann. §20-3-150 was amended in June 2002. It now reads,

> For purposes of this subsection, and unless otherwise agreed to in writing by the parties, "continued cohabitation" means the supported spouse resides with another person in a romantic relationship for a period of ninety or more consecutive days. The court may determine that a continued cohabitation exists if there is evidence that the supported spouse lives with another person for periods of less than ninety days and the two periodically separate in order to circumvent the ninety-day requirement.

There was a lively debate in the appellate courts about this issue for years, but the General Assembly ended the debate with this law. Former spouses cannot cohabitate with a romantic partner if they want to keep their alimony. **Payors who are paying alimony should keep tabs on what their ex-spouses are up to if they object to paying alimony.**

Alimony is based on the concept that, in the traditional case, the husband has a legal duty to provide the wife with the same lifestyle she had during the marriage. This standard is somewhat bizarre, in that only the wealthiest couples can continue to enjoy the same lifestyle separately after divorce, and even the wealthy often cannot do it. An affluent couple earning $200,000 or more per year who divorced and live in separate homes, with three children in private schools, cannot each maintain the same lifestyle as they did prior to the divorce. Nevertheless, that is one of the stated goals of the law. In recent cases, however, the courts seem to have placed less emphasis on this factor.

Typically, the young wife of a young doctor earning $100,000 per year does not yet have the lifestyle she hoped to have. When her husband runs off with the nurse, the wife who put him through medical school is only entitled to the lifestyle she had during the marriage, not the lifestyle she hoped to have one day. Therefore, her alimony will be based on the husband's current income, although the court may take into account his future income. This is where the judge's discretion, fault and the skills of the lawyer play a significant role in arriving at higher alimony for the wife or lower alimony for the husband.

Modification of Alimony

A spouse's alimony, once fixed by the court, is not modifiable if the payor's income increases. This may seem unfair, but the courts seek to balance the interests of the parties and to encourage the payee to seek employment. Alimony is modifiable if there is a material or substantial change in the payee's circumstances, for example, if he or she becomes ill or is injured and cannot work or loses a job through no fault of his or her own.

What about the ex-spouse who is awarded alimony and becomes successfully employed? Is he or she punished for his or her success? Yes and no. If the parties anticipate that the payee will become employed or remain employed and his or her income, real or potential, is taken into account in establishing the amount of alimony, there is no change of circumstance. The payee's alimony is not decreased on account of anticipated success. Where the agreement or court order explicitly or implicitly recognizes that the payee will have income, the payor cannot seek a reduction because the payee has in fact earned what was expected.

But suppose the agreement or order is silent? Suppose the husband thought the wife would not be employed, or at least not so successfully? Suppose the wife exceeded her own expectations? These are sometimes contentious cases.

Once again, the role of the lawyer in drafting the agreement is critical. If a payee's future earnings will or may be an issue, the wife's counsel ought to consider a provision that alimony cannot be reduced so long as the wife's income does not exceed a certain amount. If the husband believes the wife will earn more and that he ought to be relieved of his obligation or have it reduced, this should be addressed in the agreement.

Good financial planning is essential to an equitable alimony plan that will stand the test of time and free the parties from future litigation. Such planning should include the payee's purchasing or retaining the right home, considering taxes, insurance, repairs, regime fees, maintenance; a reliable automobile and future replacements (taxes, insurance, repairs); health insurance (an increasingly difficult cost to predict); debts (unknown or unconsidered liens, judgments, credit card bills and lawsuits can wreak havoc on any plan); past tax liabilities; and assets with negative values, such as timeshares or closely held corporate stock, just to mention a few.

The role of the lawyer in some of these financial matters is necessarily limited. Lawyers are not financial advisors, accountants, tax experts, appraisers, engineers or realtors. The parties must either rely on their own judgment or retain professionals to advise them. If the payee is unsure about the value or condition of the house where he or she plans to live, it should be inspected by a competent engineer and appraised by a competent appraiser. All questions of value and taxes must be answered by someone competent to do so.

The same thing is true of health insurance. Alimony cases can sometimes turn on the payee's present and future health and health insurance and medical needs. Options should be explored carefully. The payee may be eligible for health insurance through her employment, or, if he or she is in good health, the payee may be able to purchase health insurance at a reasonable cost. The payee may be entitled to the benefits of a federal law, COBRA (Consolidated Omnibus Budget Reconciliation Act), which requires health insurers to keep former spouses insured for three years after the divorce. But COBRA coverage may be impractical because the cost of the premium is not regulated and may be too high. These are technical matters that vary from case to case. For more information on COBRA, see www.dol.gov/ebsa.

The Role of Life Insurance

Another myth that needs to be exploded is that the payor is required to provide life insurance so that in the event of the payor's death, the payee's alimony will be protected. Life insurance is an important tool in all financial planning, and definitely should be an integral part of an alimony settlement, but South Carolina law does not provide much protection for the dependent spouse in this area.

Because a husband's obligation to pay alimony terminates on his death, there is no common law duty for a husband to provide life insurance in the event of a divorce, nor could the Family Court award it. The alimony statute, §20-3-130 S.C. Code, attempted to address this problem by providing that the Family Court "may require a spouse, with due consideration of the cost of the premiums, insurance plans carried by the parties during marriage, insurability of the payor spouse, the probable economic condition of the supported spouse upon the death of the payor spouse, and any other factors the court may deem relevant, to carry and maintain life insurance so as to assure support of a spouse beyond the death of the payor spouse."

However, the Court of Appeals and the Supreme Court have limited this statute by holding that there must be "special circumstances" to justify a judge in ordering life insurance to secure alimony. The courts look to the payee's need for security, i.e., his or her provable economic condition, in the event of the payor's death; the parties' age, health, income earning ability and assets; and the payor's ability to pay the premiums, his or her insurability, cost of premiums and insurance carried by the parties during the marriage.

Thus it is unclear exactly what the circumstances are that will allow a judge to order life insurance. The Supreme Court rejected the notion, advanced by the Court of Appeals, that a court-mandated requirement for life insurance "is the exception, not the rule." (Does this mean it should be the rule?) This is an area that calls for keen negotiation between the parties with the advice of competent accountants and life insurance agents. The payor may have a paid-up policy or term insurance (say for another fifteen years) at a relatively low cost. The payee may be able to buy a life insurance policy on the payor's life and pay for it herself, if it makes economic sense to do so. Or the payor may be willing to leave money to a trust that will support the wife for her life and then go to the children.

Alimony payments are enforced by the Family Court. The court may order the support payments to be paid directly to the wife or through the court. The Family Court rules provide for automatic enforcement of alimony payments that are paid through the court. The clerk of court is required to perform monthly reviews of all accounts paid through the court and to issue a rule to show cause for contempt whenever an account is in arrears.

Thus alimony cases before, during and after divorce revolve around fault, the age, health and ability of the payee to support himself or herself, the payor's financial capacity, financial and tax planning, property division and other factors.

Chapter 4

Division of Property

He taught me housekeeping; when I divorce I keep the house.

—Zsa Zsa Gabor

My luck changed because of the little woman. I made my first million, and I owe it all to the little woman. She was two inches high. I sold her to a circus and made a million dollars.

—Dave Ketchum

The division of property in a divorce or separation—referred to in South Carolina as "apportionment" of marital property—is a relatively new concept. Historically, property belonged to the title owner, usually the husband. Prior to the adoption of the doctrine of equitable appointment in the 1970s, wives were not entitled to any portion of the property acquired during the marriage. The law has changed dramatically in the last thirty years. In 1986, the General Assembly adopted a comprehensive statute, the Equitable Appointment of Marital Property Act, S.C. Code §20-7-471 to §20-7- 479 (www.scstatehouse.net/code/t20c007.doc or www.straighttalkscdivorce.com), which is similar to property division statutes around the country, especially in the East. Many of the western states, notably California, are "community property" jurisdictions rather than equitable appointment jurisdictions like South Carolina.

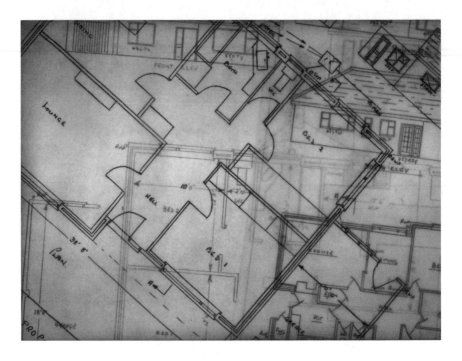

What Is Marital Property?

The concept of equitable appointment holds that at the time of divorce or other marital litigation, such as separation, each spouse has the right to claim his or her "vested special equity and ownership right" in the marital property. Strictly speaking, "marital property" does not exist until marital litigation is filed. Thus, two spouses cannot live together and litigate the issue of who owns what. Equitable appointment is based on the concept that marriage is an economic partnership and when the partnership dissolves, each partner is entitled to a fair share of the assets based on fourteen specific factors, such as length of marriage and contribution to the marital estate. Thus, as in all matters in Family Court, judges have a great deal of discretion in apportioning marital property.

Marital property is all property of any kind or description acquired by the parties during the marriage and that is owned when litigation begins, except gifts, inheritances, property acquired in exchange for gifts or inheritances, the increase in value of nonmarital property (unless the other spouse helped increase the value) and property excluded by a prenuptial agreement. Title is irrelevant. The type of property is irrelevant. If the husband is a partner in a business, his partnership interest is marital property. **All property acquired by the parties during the marriage and owned on the date of filing of marital litigation is presumed to be marital property, unless it falls into one of the exceptions.**

Thus, the marital home (no matter who is on the deed or whose name it is in), automobiles, investments, stocks and bonds, money market accounts, bank accounts, furniture, art, collectibles, pensions, retirement funds (except Social Security), military pensions, businesses, partnership investments, stocks in corporations, LLC memberships, leases, options, copyrights, patents, royalties, legal claims and lawsuits (such as personal injury or worker's compensation claims), money owed to one of the spouses, life insurance cash value, tax refunds, gifts between spouses during the marriage (jewelry, Christmas and birthday presents), stock options and even cemetery plots and animals are all marital property. If it is "property," it is marital property. Engagement rings are nonmarital property, because they were acquired before the marriage. If a party claims property is nonmarital, he or she has the burden of proving it.

Technically, property acquired after the date of filing of the marital litigation is nonmarital, but if it is acquired with marital funds, it is marital. The passive appreciation or depreciation in marital assets occurring after a separation or after filing is marital. Thus, if the value of the stocks in a Merrill Lynch account goes up, the increase is marital.

The increase in value of nonmarital property has presented the courts with difficult problems. Suppose a woman marries a man and moves into his house. This house, even though it might be the "marital home" for thirty years, remains the husband's nonmarital property. In *Ray v. Ray*, the parties moved into the marital home in 1971. They substantially remodeled it. In 1976, the husband acquired the title as a gift from his stepmother. The couple separated in 1985. The wife not only lived in the home, but also kept it up and cleaned it. Nevertheless, the court held as follows:

> The only evidence of transmutation after the husband acquired title is that the parties lived in the house for nine years. As we have noted, the mere use of non-marital property to support the marriage, without some additional evidence of intent to treat it as property of the marriage, is not sufficient to establish transmutation.

Transmutation

Nonmarital property can become marital property if it is "transmuted" into marital property. Transmutation is a confusing concept, to say the least. It is easy to state, but difficult to apply. Transmutation is ultimately a matter of intent based on the facts of each case. The spouse claiming transmutation must produce objective evidence showing that the parties themselves regarded the property as common property of the marriage. Such evidence could include placing the property in joint name, gifting the property to the other spouse, using the property exclusively for marital purposes, using marital funds to build equity, paying off a mortgage or exchanging the property for marital property. However, the mere use of separate property to support the marriage, without additional evidence, is not sufficient to establish transmutation. Facts vary from case to case. Where a wife refused to jointly title the house so the husband could use it for collateral for a loan, the court held that this was proof that she had no intent to transmute it.

A party can transmute a pension fund into marital property. In *Murphy v. Murphy*, the Supreme Court held that after Mr. Murphy's retirement, the parties agreed upon a game plan whereby the nonmarital portion of the pension fund was commingled with the portion earned subsequent to the marriage, and the entire pension fund was used to support the marriage. Mrs. Murphy waived her right to survivor benefits in the whole pension fund so that the parties could receive accelerated retirement payments during the marriage. The nonmarital portion of the pension fund was transmuted into a marital asset when the parties utilized the entire pension fund in support of the marriage.

The marital home is always subject to being transmuted, and judges are more willing to find transmutation where the marital home is involved than when income from other types of property is used in support of the marriage. For example, in *Peterkin v. Peterkin*, the Supreme Court reversed the trial court for not finding that the acreage surrounding the marital home, in addition to the home itself, had been transmuted.

The most typical evidence to show transmutation of the marital home is the discharge of indebtedness against it. In *Frank v. Frank*, the Court of Appeals held that the marital home, which was owned by the wife prior to the marriage, was transmuted into marital property when both parties signed a promissory note securing a mortgage on the house, and therefore both parties were liable for the discharge of the debt. However, it is important to know whether the discharge of debt is a preexisting indebtedness. Adding new debt to the marital home by mortgaging the property and using the proceeds for marital purposes has been held not to transmute the property, because the loan proceeds did not enhance the value of or build equity in the property.

The Family Court must make a factual finding as to whether nonmarital property has been transmuted to marital property. If it does not, the court has no jurisdiction over the property. If it has been transmuted, that does not mean it must be divided in any particular way. The trial judge can still consider the source of the property and give that great weight in deciding how to apportion it.[1] It may be marital property, but that is only the first part of the analysis. Transmutation only puts the property "in the pot" or "on the table." A million-dollar house inherited late in the marriage, although transmuted, should not be equally divided.

Nonmarital property can become marital property when it becomes so commingled as to be untraceable. The phrase "so commingled as to be untraceable" is all-important, because mere commingling of funds does not automatically make them marital. In *Brooks v. Brooks*, the wife deposited $10,000 from an inheritance into a separate account, along with $1,000 of joint funds. The Family Court included the entire $11,000 in the marital estate, but the Court of Appeals reversed the decision, holding that mere commingling did not transmute.

Appreciation of nonmarital property can be marital. S.C. Code §20-7-473 defines "marital property" as "all real and personal property which has been acquired by the parties during the marriage and which is owned as of the date of filing or commencement of marital litigation, except any increase in value in nonmarital property, except to the extent that the increase resulted directly or indirectly from efforts of the other spouse during the marriage." Thus, the increase in value of nonmarital property does not always have to be transmuted. It could arguably be marital.

The problem, of course, is to determine the extent that the increase resulted from "efforts of the other spouse." A homemaker's indirect contribution, i.e., raising the children and taking care of the home, may be sufficient to make the appreciation of the nonmarital home marital.

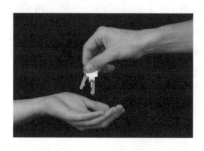

Dividing or apportioning a marital property is a four-step process: Identifying the marital property (What is it?), valuing the marital property (How much is it worth?), apportioning the property (Who should get it?) and distributing the property (How to divide it?).

Identifying Marital Property

In most cases, identifying marital property is simple and straightforward. Both spouses know they have a jointly titled home, retirement plans, bank and stock accounts, cars, furniture and other assets. But in some cases, identifying marital property is more difficult. One spouse may be hiding assets. This is why hiring a competent lawyer and CPA is so important, and why a complete investigation may need to be done. The obvious sources are tax returns, financial statements and loan applications submitted to a bank, a search of the public records for deeds, personal property or security interests in property and business records. If one spouse is suspicious that the tax returns are not genuine, one can obtain tax returns directly from the IRS (use IRS Form 4506), receive signed financial statements and loan applications directly from the bank and have a CPA examine business records, credit cards, bank records and money market accounts. Sometimes one spouse does not realize that the other spouse has stock options, performance stock or other little-known types of compensation as part of his or her compensation package. I was in a case where a husband tried to hide a large amount of cash by intentionally overpaying his taxes! Who would think that the money—which would ultimately be refunded to him—was hidden at the IRS?

A comprehensive history or chronology of the marriage is always helpful, because one spouse may have a valuable retirement account or pension from a job he or she had long ago. Money could have been left behind in a bank or credit union in a city where the parties formerly resided.

Legal claims are marital property. If your spouse was in a serious automobile accident, he or she may settle that claim for a great deal of money one day. The Family Court can retain jurisdiction to divide those funds.

Sometimes it is not clear whether something of value is property or not. For example, in *Mallet v. Mallet*, the court held that termination benefits payable to the husband when he ceased to be employed were not marital property because the benefits were based on the husband's earnings in the year prior to his termination, which could be long after the divorce.

A professional degree is not property under South Carolina law. As Roy G. Blount put it, "Doctors and lawyers must go to school for years and years, often with little sleep and with great sacrifice to their first wives." The fact that the wife put the husband through medical school is a factor in dividing property and awarding alimony, but the degree itself is not property that can be divided. (In New York, a medical degree can be divided. This is an example of how the states differ in their treatment of property division issues.) The value of a husband's interest in his professional (medical, dental, accounting, legal practice) association is property included in the marital estate, even though ownership in a professional practice is restricted to duly licensed members of the profession. One spouse cannot be awarded an interest in the professional association of the other spouse, as she or he is not a member of the profession, but the value of the spouse's interest in the association should be considered when computing the total value of the marital estate.

Valuation of Marital Property

Valuation can be simple, or it can be one of the most complex tasks facing lawyers and judges. Most spouses have a good idea what their homes, automobiles, furniture, stocks and bonds, retirement funds and investments are worth. CPAs are sometimes needed to place a value on the marital portion of a retirement fund when part of it was earned prior to the marriage and part during the marriage. Funds obtained in earlier years may be more valuable than funds or stocks obtained in recent years. Real estate, furniture, art and collectibles can all be appraised by experts if necessary. Where the parties cannot agree on values, the judge must listen to testimony, usually from expert appraisers, and make a decision about the value.

Another problem in divorce cases is valuing the family business. Where the parties own a store, a restaurant, a dental or medical practice, a car dealership, an insurance agency or innumerable other businesses together, there may be a vast difference in the values the parties place on it. Nevertheless, experts can value any business. They do it all the time, not only in divorce cases, but also in determining a reasonable sales price for tax and estate purposes and for loans.

South Carolina is conservative in its approach to valuation of businesses. Our courts have been careful to limit the value of "goodwill," an especially difficult thing to place a value on. Goodwill has been described as

> the advantage or benefit, which is acquired by an establishment, beyond the mere value of the capital stock, funds, or property employed therein, in consequence of general public patronage and encouragement, which it receives from constant or habitual customers, on account of its local position, or common celebrity, or reputation for skill or affluence, or punctuality, or from other accidental circumstances or necessities, or even from ancient partialities or prejudices.

In other words, if Frank's Hot Dog Stand sells especially good hot dogs, has a good reputation and makes a lot of money, it is obviously worth more than the stand, the lease, the appliances and the supply of hot dogs. But how to place a value on goodwill?

Generally, the courts value a business at fair market value as an ongoing business not in a distress sale, and not just tangible assets. This valuation method includes "realizable goodwill" as a marital asset, but South Carolina courts are extremely cautious when measuring goodwill. The court will consider the net asset value, the fair market value for the stock of the business and earnings or investment value.[2]

Valuation issues can many times be resolved by evidence already available, such as financial statements that one or both of the parties submitted to a bank (be sure to have your lawyer subpoena the original from the bank) or by a valuation of the business performed by an expert for purpose of a sale. Some businesses and industries use a "rule of thumb." For example, dental and medical practices might be sold for one year's gross earnings. Occasionally, businesses will have buy-sell agreements where the actual value, or a formula, is set out in the partnership, corporate or LLC agreement. The courts are not bound by these agreements, but they do provide strong evidence of value.

When the husband has a stream of income from a business and therefore goodwill, the South Carolina courts hold that the wife may still benefit through an award of alimony. But if the wife is barred from alimony because she committed adultery, she simply loses out. The Supreme Court held in *Berry v. Berry* that "the preclusion of an alimony award to a spouse cannot be used to increase an equitable distribution award…Where a spouse is adjudged guilty of adultery, an increase in an equitable distribution award would contravene the public policy considerations manifested in the alimony-barring statute."

Marital property must be considered together with marital debt. Sometimes this issue can be contentious, as the dependent spouse many times is not aware of the liability side of the marital ledger. A couple may appear to be affluent, live in an expensive home and enjoy a luxurious lifestyle, but at the same time may be saddled with enormous debt. The credit card debt, equity line, mortgage, liens, judgments and outstanding bills must be paid or one party or the other must assume responsibility for the debt.

Apportioning Marital Property

After the property has been identified and valued, it must be apportioned. §20-7-472 S.C. Code sets forth the criteria to do so. The factors are, generally

- the length of the marriage;
- fault;
- the direct and indirect contributions of each spouse, including the contributions of a homemaker;
- income earning potential;
- potential for further acquisition of assets;
- opportunity for the parties to acquire wealth;
- need for education or training;
- other (nonmarital) assets;
- vested retirement benefits;
- whether support was awarded;
- who will get the family home;
- tax consequences of the apportionment;
- support obligations from a prior marriage;
- debts and liabilities;
- custody arrangements and obligations;
- and such other relevant factors as the trial court shall expressly state in its order.

Judge Cureton wrote in *Jones v. Jones* that "we cannot develop a precise mathematical formula to govern our Family Court judges in making such awards…we must rely, therefore, on our Family Court judges whose mature judgments we accord great deference." He wrote again in *Josey v. Josey*, "Perhaps a Family Court's most difficult task in distributing the marital estate is to determine an appropriate division. The amount should bear a reasonable relationship to the relative direct and indirect contributions of the parties to the acquisition and maintenance of the marital property."

The Family Court has wide discretion in distributing marital property. Trial judges are given wide latitude in devising practical solutions to the myriad problems presented in divorce cases, and generally their decisions will not be disturbed on appeal. The appellate courts look to the fairness of the overall apportionment and whether the end result is equitable. Minor errors not materially affecting the overall division are ignored.

Stuckey concludes in *Marital Litigation in South Carolina,*

> Although neither the case decisions nor the Equitable Apportionment of Marital Property Act say so directly, the results in cases involving long marriages would lead one to predict that, absent special circumstances, marital property will be divided on a fifty-fifty basis, at least where the wife has been a homemaker, and perhaps, where she has made some other contribution to the accumulation of marital assets.

Most South Carolina lawyers agree that as a practical matter, if not as a legal matter, judges presume a fifty-fifty division in long or even moderately long marriages. Of course, some spouses, especially those who feel wronged, want more than 50 percent. As comedian Jackie Mason once said, "Anyone who thinks that marriage is a fifty-fifty proposition doesn't understand women or fractions."

Numerous cases state that fault is not to be given great weight. However, fault is a wild card in Family Court and can be a very important factor. A husband's drinking, for example, can constitute marital misconduct that damaged the economic status of the parties. In *Woodside v. Woodside*, the Court of Appeals held:

> We believe that the conduct factor becomes important in equitable distribution when the conduct of one party to the marriage is such that it throws upon the other party marital burdens beyond the norms to be expected in the marital relationship...marriage is an economic partnership to which both spouses contribute. When the conduct of one of the parties causes the other party to assume more than his or

her share of the partnership load, it is appropriate that such
misconduct should affect the distribution of the property of
the marriage.

Or as one wag aptly noted, "She cried, and the judge wiped her tears
with my checkbook."

In *Sharpe v. Sharpe*, the Court of Appeals addressed whether attempted
murder should have some effect on the equitable apportionment of
the marital property. In all fairness to Mrs. Sharpe, she was only
guilty of conspiracy to murder her husband, and the result might
have been different had she succeeded in killing her husband. Mr.
Sharpe was guilty of post-separation adultery. The wife admitted that
she had conspired with others to kill her husband, but the attempt
failed because the husband got wind of the conspiracy. Mrs. Sharpe
still received 35 percent of the marital estate.

Awarding the Marital Home

Judges can consider the desirability of awarding the family home as
a part of the apportionment. The Supreme Court recently redefined
the law on how to apportion the home, giving new meaning to Lewis
Grizzard's quote, "Instead of getting married again, I'm going to find
a woman I don't like and give her a house." In *Wooten v. Wooten*, the
Supreme Court held that the award of the marital home was not based
solely on dollars, but also was based on the welfare of the parties.

> The Family Court should consider not only financial factors
> (including tax consequences, if any) affecting the distribution
> of the marital home, but also the physical and emotional
> well-being of each spouse as it relates to the marital home.
> In other words, decisions relating to the equitable distribution
> of the marital home should not always be based solely or

primarily on a cold, rational calculation of dollars and cents. The Family Court is free to consider other, less tangible factors asserted by a spouse, weighing those in concert with the financial impact on the parties.

The court has said that all sorts of factors come in to play, such as emancipated children living in or visiting the home, keeping the home in the family and the wife's security.

Courts also consider the tax consequences of property division. Many litigants are adamant that an asset should only be considered in after-tax dollars. This, however, is not the law. If an asset has not been sold or its sale is not imminent, the tax consequences of a possible sale should not be considered. Where, however, the asset will be sold as part of the court-ordered apportionment, the court should consider the tax consequences. Where a party incurs tax penalties that should not have been incurred, that party can be made to bear the burden of that payment.

Liens, encumbrances and debts should all be considered. The court should ensure that the debts were incurred for the benefit of both parties during the marriage. There is a presumption that the debt of either spouse incurred prior to marital litigation is a marital debt and must be factored in the apportionment. This presumption is rebuttable, but all charges at Victoria's Secret should be carefully scrutinized.

The husband's greater earning potential is an important factor in apportioning property, as he will acquire assets in the future and a homemaker-wife will not.

Where one spouse's family contributed disproportionately to the marital estate, the court may award a higher percentage to that spouse. In *Bungener v. Bungener*, it was held that the husband, who "with the assistance of his mother" contributed almost all of the marital support for the family, was properly awarded more than half of the marital estate. In *Sexton v. Sexton*, the Court of Appeals reversed what it viewed to be an excessive award to the wife, citing among other facts, "The husband and his family contributed substantially all of the labor to build the house…the husband's father advanced construction costs…the fact that a substantial portion of the value of the house is attributed to contributions made by husband's family should be a consideration in this case."

The spouse seeking **more than 50 percent** has a heavy burden of proving the amount, as **judges tend to resist deviating from fifty-fifty divisions.**

The Family Court has a great deal of latitude in this area. The court may use any reasonable means in dividing the property and can direct a party to assign or deed property and execute a note, a mortgage or any other document. It can order a public sale or a monetary award. Orders of the Family Court requiring a party to pay money are money judgments like any other money judgment. Money judgments currently draw interest at 12.25 percent (2007).

Judges do all they can to sever all financial relationships between divorcing spouses. The judge should attempt to "sever all entangling legal relations" and resolve all issues so that "disputed and irritants do not linger." One spouse will not ordinarily be awarded a percentage of a closely held corporation owned by the other spouse. As management of property is difficult "between persons at odds after divorce," it is better simply to divide property and award discrete properties to each party, where possible.

In dividing retirement plans and pensions, if the pension is small, it is wise to apportion it to one party. If an apportionment can be accomplished without dividing a pension, this should certainly be considered. Pension plans are designed to keep money out of the hands of creditors, and so they cannot be assigned or alienated except in special circumstances. One such special circumstance is in a divorce, when a Family Court can require payment from a pension plan as part of the apportionment of the marital estate. A special order is needed to divide certain retirement plans. A Qualified Domestic Relations Order

(QDRO) creates or recognizes the existence of the other spouse's interest in a pension or retirement fund as an "alternate payee." The best way to obtain a QDRO that a retirement plan administrator will acknowledge is to obtain a form from the plan administrator or to retain a lawyer knowledgeable in the area. Family Courts may divide the pension or retirement funds and direct that a QDRO be issued.

Once the court issues an order, there is a judgment of record, which operates as a lien. If a party will not transfer property, disobeys an order or leaves the state, the Family Court has the power to appoint a trustee, a receiver or a sequestrator to make the required transfer.

Chapter 5

Custody and Visitation

> When I meet a man I ask myself, is this the man I want my children to spend their weekends with?
>
> —Rita Rudman

> My wife used to always say to me, "Why can't a woman have the same ambitions as a man?" I think you're right. And maybe I've learned that much, but by the same token, I'd like to know what law is it that says a woman is a better parent simply by virtue of her sex.
>
> —Dustin Hoffman in *Kramer vs. Kramer*

Contested custody cases are the death penalty cases of Family Court. When ordinary people are fighting over the health and well-being—indeed, the very lives of their children—the stakes are high and compromise sometimes becomes impossible, as in abuse and neglect cases. These are the worst cases Family Court judges see. Everyone wants to avoid a contested custody case: the parents because of the high stakes and high costs (financially and psychologically); the lawyers because of the stress, difficulty and general unprofitability of such cases; the counselors, psychologists and pediatricians because of the risk of serious damage to the children and family; and judges because they do not want the responsibility for the well-being of children if it can be resolved by the parents.

Thus, **the culture of the Family Court is opposed to the litigation of custody cases and does all it can to avoid them.**

Contesting parents are told by their attorneys to work out custody problems with their spouses directly or through counselors. Judges frequently order parents to attend programs designed to resolve the conflict.

The settlement of a custody case almost always takes place outside the Family Court where legal rule prevails. These settlements may arise in a therapeutic setting, from negotiations between the parties and their lawyers, through mediation or from a counseling environment, where the parties are influenced by the values and beliefs of lawyers, social workers, guardians, counselors, mediators, psychologists and others who may or may not have the slightest idea what the law is or what the judges in that part of the state actually decide in court.

This is not necessarily bad. In fact, it is probably good, because the law on custody and what is actually good for a particular family do not necessarily coincide. Few people argue any longer that a father should only see his children every other weekend, yet that was the law not so long ago and still is in some counties.

Most custody cases in South Carolina are settled by the parties on familiar lines: the mother is given "sole custody" (or simply "custody") and the father is given "reasonable and liberal" visitation rights. Standard visitation varies from judge to judge, but some judges have developed a standard visitation form they attach to their orders. See www.straighttalkscdivorce.com.

The appellate cases describe standard visitation as every other weekend (Friday at 6:00 p.m. to Sunday at 6:00 p.m.), several weeks in the summer and alternating or split holidays (Easter, Thanksgiving, Christmas, Labor Day, etc.) See, for example, *Woodside v. Woodside* and *Johns v. Johns*. But visitation can be tailored to individual needs. A truck driver, whose schedule is erratic, or a doctor, whose call

The settlement of a custody case almost always takes place outside the Family Court where legal rule prevails.

schedule changes, needs flexibility. Unfortunately, some ex-wives and some Family Court judges are not flexible. Thus, it behooves a noncustodial parent to bargain for all the time and flexibility he can get, rather than go to court and be told by a judge, "Here is my standard visitation schedule. Good luck."

Most fathers are satisfied for mothers to have custody of the children, so long as they have reasonable access or visitation and their ex-wives are willing to listen to their suggestions on raising the children. This simple concept is usually self-policing, because fathers can have more influence when they actually participate in their children's lives and mothers are ordinarily happy for the assistance both in time and money. Thus, mercifully, most divorced couples work it out without reference to the law or lawyers.

Some people, however, cannot work it out. Contested custody cases fall into familiar categories:

- angry men who want to hurt their ex-wives by seeking custody or alienating the children;
- angry women who want to hurt their ex-husbands by withholding or alienating the children;
- a spouse genuinely protecting the children from an abusive, dangerous or unsuitable parent;
- a spouse (usually the husband) trying to get custodial time in order to pay less child support;
- men who genuinely believe that they are the primary parent and sincerely want custody;
- men or women who want "true joint custody," i.e., 50 percent of the time and true joint decision making;

- men who want their version of joint custody (namely, mother does most of the work, but father gets to tell mother what to do and how to do it);
- and relocation cases (mom wants to move away and take the children).

Each of these cases has a legal, financial and psychological dynamic of its own.

Custody Agreement

Thus, parties negotiate all sorts of agreements that may or may not have any legal meaning under South Carolina law. Many lay people, and some lawyers, use words like "legal custody" (meaning essentially "custody," i.e., the right to make decisions about a child as well as having primary physical possession of them) and "physical custody" (meaning the amount of time the child lives with a parent, basically visitation). South Carolina law does not forbid agreements using these words, but the concepts are certainly not clear in the law. As Professor Stuckey points out in *Marital Litigation*, "Neither South Carolina statutes nor cases define the differences between legal and physical custody or the numerous other types of potential custody arrangements." According to Beaufort attorney Peter L. Fuge, "Our appellate courts used such terms as 'joint legal custody,' 'primary custody,' 'secondary custody,' 'shared custody,' 'divided custody,' 'sole custody,' 'joint custody arrangement,' 'primary placement,' and 'primary physical custody,' without providing any legal definitions."

The Supreme Court encourages people to settle their differences. In *Ford v. Ford*, the court held, "The rule is that contracts between spouses as to the custody of children will be recognized unless the welfare of the children requires a different disposition." A party reneging on an agreement must show that the welfare of the children required the court to set aside the agreement. The court will consider whether the agreement was equitable and in the best interests of the children at the time it was entered into. If it is deemed to be so, the court will consider whether there has been a sufficient change of conditions so that the agreement was not under the circumstances prevailing at the time of the trial, a proper one in the best interests of the children. Thus, if the agreement entered into by the parties—regardless of the terminology or "parenting plan"—is fair and in the best interest of the children, it will be enforced by the courts.

A parent challenging a custody agreement has the burden of proving that the agreement was improperly created, was not in the children's best interests or that there has been a substantial change of circumstances affecting the welfare of the children since the agreement was signed.

Where there is no agreement or order, the law of South Carolina holds that parents are equal before the law when it comes to custody, according to S.C. Code Ann. §20-7-100:

> The mother and father are the joint natural guardians of their minor children and are equally charged with the welfare and education of their minor children and the care and management of the estate of their minor children; and the father and mother have equal power, rights, and duties, and neither parent has any right paramount to the right of the other concerning the custody of the minor or the control of the services or the earnings of the minor or any other matter affecting the minor.

Thus, assuming no court order is in place, theoretically, any parent can pick up one day and move the children to another state. Of course, in practice, the other parent could initiate litigation in South Carolina, the children's "home state," and the Family Court could order the children returned.

In order for the Family Court to award custody, it must have jurisdiction over a child under the age of eighteen years. Once a child reaches his eighteenth birthday, he is no longer a minor child.

Ordinarily, custody cases involve South Carolina residents who are divorcing, but occasionally parents will move to South Carolina and leave the other parent behind in another state. If one parent and the children live in South Carolina, South Carolina will ordinarily decide the issue, but there are exceptions. For example, if one parent takes the children from their home and moves to South Carolina without the other parent's agreement, South Carolina will likely defer to the children's home state. The rules involving interstate custody are complex and are governed by the Uniform Child Custody Jurisdiction Act, §20-7-782 to 830. S.C. Code (www.judicial.state.sc.us) and the Federal Parental Kidnapping Prevention Act of 1980 (PKPA), 28 U.S.C. §1738 A (www.amber-net.org/statues/federal.pdf). Where parties were divorced in another state and one of the parents still resides in that state, South Carolina may also defer to the state that originally issued the custody order. When a parent leaves South Carolina with the children and relocates, South Carolina continues to have jurisdiction over the children until the other parent has resided in the new state for six months.

Under South Carolina law, there is "sole custody" and there is "joint custody." Sole custody was described previously. "Split custody" is a variation of sole custody where one parent has sole custody of one child and the other parent has sole custody of the other child.

Joint Custody

"Joint" or "shared" custody comes in a variety of forms. The courts see joint custody as a more equal or generous sharing of time and a sharing of decision-making authority. Joint custody can range from a literal fifty-fifty division of time to as little as the traditional visitation schedule, and anything in between. Many joint custody agreements give the mother the majority of the time, but award the father extended visitation on the weekends (Thursday after school to Sunday evening, or Friday after school to school on Monday), plus one or two overnights on the "off weeks," i.e, weeks with no weekend visitation, custody or "custodial time," plus one half of all holidays and one half of the summer months. When parents opt for a fifty-fifty division, some lawyers refer to the arrangement as "divided" or "alternating" custody.

The South Carolina courts have not been friendly to joint custody. In *Mixson v. Mixson*, the Supreme Court held that, while parents might agree on joint custody, the courts will not order joint custody except under exceptional circumstances. "The best interest and welfare of the children demand that divided custody should be avoided if possible, and it will not be approved except under exceptional circumstances or for strong and convincing reasons." Divided custody is usually harmful to and not conducive to the best interest and welfare of the children. The court held that "dividing the custody of a child between contending parties" and "the custody of a child in brief alternating periods between estranged and quarrelsome persons" is unacceptable. The court stated,

> Ordinarily it is not conducive to the best interests and welfare of a child to be shifted and shuttled back and forth in alternate brief periods between contending parties, particularly during the school term. Furthermore, such an arrangement is likely to cause confusion, interfere with proper training and discipline of the child, make the child the basis of many quarrels between its custodians, render its life unhappy and discontented, and prevent it from living a normal life.

The court in *Mixson* reversed a decision by the trial judge to award joint custody, finding no exceptional circumstances to justify the order.

Despite a widespread belief to the contrary, the South Carolina courts have not been friendly to joint custody.

Despite a widespread belief to the contrary, the law has changed but little since 1969. In *Parris v. Parris*, the Supreme Court referred to "our long-standing prohibition against joint custody." In 1996, the General Assembly, apparently seeking to overturn or modify *Mixson* and *Parris*, amended §20-7-420 of the S.C. Code to give Family Court judges the authority "to order joint or divided custody where the court finds it in the best interest of the child," omitting the requirement of "exceptional circumstances." But the courts seem not to have understood §20-7-420 this way, and continue to be wary of joint custody.

In 2000, the Court of Appeals made a slight concession to joint custody in *Paparella v. Paparella*, where the court held that a "concerned, loving" father involved in the "day-to-day activities" of the children was entitled to more time:

> Under the circumstances, we agree with the father that he should be allowed more visitation with the children. Pursuant to the Family Court order, the father's visits are twelve days apart. Therefore, we modify the visitation schedule to provide as follows: during the school year, the father will have the children every other weekend, beginning after school on Friday and ending when they return to school Monday morning. Then on the Thursday preceding the weekend when the father does not have visitation, the father will have the children after school until they return to school Friday morning. Also on the Tuesday following the weekend when he does not have visitation, the father will have them after school until they return to school Wednesday morning. This will permit the father to see his children more often. The father's summer visitation is expanded so that he has the children half of the children's summer vacation.

The court encouraged the parties "to consider permitting the parent not in physical custody to have the children when the other parent is working."

This was not joint custody by any definition, but it was a recognition that fathers truly involved in their children's lives are entitled to more time with their children after a divorce. However, many Family Court judges will not award joint custody if one of the parties objects.

When the parents cannot agree, the Family Court will decide which parent will have custody and which parent will have visitation, and how much visitation. As we have seen, a court cannot order joint custody absent exceptional circumstances. In order to arrive at a decision, the court is governed by "the best interests of the child." This may seem obvious, but well into the eighteenth and nineteenth centuries, fathers essentially owned their children, were entitled to their services as laborers and were routinely granted custody. Indeed, in order to get a mother's children back from an abusive father, the legendary Charleston lawyer James L. Petigru had the court issue a writ of *habeas corpus* to return the children to the mother! §20-7-100 S.C. Code provides that "the welfare of the minor shall be the first consideration and the court having jurisdiction shall determine all questions concerning the guardianship of the minor." But as the Supreme Court declared in *Ford v. Ford*, "The difficulty is not in the recognition of the foregoing principles, but in the application thereof to the facts of the case, and determining what is for the best interests of the children involves a consideration of all of the circumstances of the particular case and, usually, many factors."

Guardians

In order to protect the best interest of a minor child in a contested custody case, the Family Court will appoint a guardian *ad litem* (GAL). In a celebrated case, *Patel v. Patel*, the Supreme Court required GALs to conduct "an independant, balanced, and impartial investigation," to review relevant documents, meet with and observe the child in the home setting, interview relevant witnesses and consider the child's wishes. Since *Patel* and a recent GAL statute, GALs are—or should be—more mindful of their duties to be fair and impartial.

There was a huge controversy in 2002 about the role of the GAL in Family Court, and the General Assembly enacted a statute to regulate the appointment, role and fees of GALS. §20-7-1545 S.C. Code now states that in a private custody case, the court may appoint a GAL only when it determines that without a GAL "the court will likely not be fully informed about the facts of the case and there is a substantial dispute which necessitates a Guardian ad Litem," or when the parties consent.

In practice, however, Family Court judges almost always appoint a GAL. The feeling on the bench apparently is "better safe than sorry," "what harm can it do?" and the GAL might be able to help resolve the conflict. The Supreme Court has described its vision of a GAL this way: "We think much of the criticism of guardians ad litem stems from the failure of the bar to recognize the proper function of a guardian ad litem. A guardian ad litem is a representative of the court appointed to assist it in properly protecting the interests of an incompetent person." A statement made by the court in *Bahr v. Galonski* is instructive:

> The requirement that the children have independent legal representation does not in any way suggest that the parents or trial court were unmindful of the children's welfare. Rather, it reflects the conviction that the children are best served by the presence of a vigorous advocate free to investigate, consult with them at length, marshal evidence, and to subpoena and cross examine witnesses. The judge cannot play this role. Properly understood, therefore, the guardian ad litem does not usurp the judge's function; he aids it.

GALs differ dramatically from case to case. GALs in private custody cases (not Department of Social Services cases) are almost always lawyers. They may be well suited to talking to children and evaluating parents, or they may be completely incompetent, biased or both. The opinion of a GAL depends on the intelligence, emotional health, experience and honesty of the particular GAL, as well as his or her personal history, prejudices and social values. An angry, single female lawyer with no children or a divorced male attorney whose wife ran off with another man may not be able to give an unbiased opinion about a custody case. Of course, there are many GALs who are intelligent and conscientious, have raised children and are fair and impartial.

GALs are required by §20-7-1549 to
- represent the best interest of the child;
- conduct a balanced and impartial investigation;
- meet with the child, parents and caregivers;
- attend court hearings;
- maintain a complete file;
- and present a "clear and comprehensive written report… regarding the child's best interest."

GALs are paid by the hour. They will almost always be asked their opinion on some aspect of a custody case (how much visitation, who the court-appointed psychologist should be and sometimes the ultimate issue of who should have custody), and both parties and their lawyers are prone to curry favor with the GAL as a kind of "junior judge." The nastier the case gets, the more time the GAL has to spend on the case, and the higher their fees. The new GAL statute forbids the GAL from making a recommendation as to the issue of custody unless requested to do so by the court.

Lawyers vigorously disagree on the usefulness of a GAL. Some lawyers and most judges view GALs as an objective person able to present an impartial view of the children's needs and interests. Other lawyers believe GALs are officious intermeddlers who serve no purpose, as they talk to the same witnesses as the lawyers, basing their opinions on nothing more than their own values, likes and dislikes. According to these lawyers, the judge will hear all the same testimony and does not need a GAL to tell him or her what the evidence means. But this debate is now irrelevant because it appears that, for better or worse, GALs are a fact of life in Family Court for the foreseeable future.

Custody Factors

The Supreme Court has held that the Family Court should consider how the custody decision will impact all areas of the child's life, including physical, psychological, spiritual, educational, familial, emotional and recreational aspects. *Davenport v. Davenport* holds that the Family Court "must assess each party's character, fitness, and attitude as they impact the child. '[T]he totality of circumstances peculiar to each case constitutes the only scale upon which the ultimate decision can be weighed.'"

The Court of Appeals held in *Pirayesh v. Pirayesh* as follows:

> In determining the best interest of a child in a custody dispute, the Family Court should consider several factors, including: who has been the primary caretaker; the conduct, attributes, and fitness of the parents; the opinions of third parties (including the guardian, expert witnesses, and the children); and the age, health, and sex of the children. Rather than merely adopting the recommendations of the guardian, the court, by its own review of all the evidence, should consider the character, fitness, attitude, and inclinations on the part of each parent as they impact the child as well as all psychological, physical, environmental, spiritual, educational, medical, family, emotional, and recreational aspects of the child's life. When determining to whom custody shall be awarded, the court should consider the circumstances of the particular case and all relevant factors must be taken into consideration.

Whatever the law in the appellate cases, judges decide which parent would be the better custodial parent based on all of the facts and circumstances of each individual case. The Rules of Evidence barely exist in custody cases. Everything you or your spouse ever did or failed to do in your life and almost everything your friends or relatives ever did will come into evidence. While attorneys have the right to object to evidence in a custody case, most objections are seen by judges as attempts to hide the truth about facts that may impinge on the health and well-being of a child. Thus, custody cases bring out the worst in everyone involved. No misdeed will go unreported. For accurate depictions of custody litigation, if not the actual trial procedure and technicalities, see the movies *Kramer vs. Kramer* (1979), starring Dustin Hoffman, Meryl Streep and Jane Alexander, and *The Good Wife* (1987), staring Rachel Ward.

The way to win a custody case in South Carolina is to be the primary parent and the better parent, as attested to by impartial witnesses— namely, the people who have been in your home and observed the raising of your children: teachers, babysitters, nannies, pediatricians, ministers or priests, Sunday school teachers, coaches and neighbors. Relying on counselors, therapists, psychologists and expert witnesses is problematic, unless these experts have treated the children prior to the litigation or they are agreed-upon—court-ordered—experts. Remember that therapists are people who delight in one-on-one, quiet, nonconfrontational therapy. A good therapist rarely makes a good expert witness. Indeed, therapists and counselors generally shrink from testifying (no pun intended). It is not their thing.

Judges tend to give great weight to the party who was the primary caregiver prior to the litigation. Ordinarily it is still the mother who maintains the house, helps more with the homework and takes the children to the doctor, sports, piano lessons and other extracurricular activities. But fathers who are the primary parents can and do win custody cases in South Carolina. In one celebrated case, *Parris v. Parris*, the Supreme Court upheld an award of custody to the father who played a more active role in the day-to-day activities of the child. The mother was a successful realtor and claimed that the award of custody to the father reflected a gender bias against working women. The National Organization for Women (NOW), the League of Women

Voters of South Carolina and other feminist groups filed an *amicus curiae* ("friend of the court") brief. The Supreme Court dismissed these allegations and held that the mother's work habits and the amount of time she spent (or failed to spend) with her son were "highly relevant." "Where, as here," the court opined, "the record reveals a pattern of one parent as primary caretaker and the other parent as the primary wage earner, it would be incomprehensible for a court to disregard this fact in awarding custody."

The court also gives great weight to the parents' relationship with their children, their future plans to raise the children and the proposed home, school and family support system. Religion can play a major role in custody cases. While some lawyers believe there are constitutional limits on the legal ability of the Family Court to use religion as a factor in custody cases, most lawyers and judges give significant weight to this factor. The parent who provides more religious training and takes church attendance more seriously tends to have a better chance of winning. In *Pountain v. Pountain*, the court chose a mother who had a history of writing bad checks and missed important medical appointments but "who professed to be a Christian" and paid for a private Christian school over a father who was an agnostic and whose new wife was also an agnostic.

Homosexuality, per se, is not sufficient cause to deny a parent custody in South Carolina. In fact, more than twenty years ago, in 1987, in *Stroman v. Williams*, the Court of Appeals rejected an argument by the heterosexual father that the lesbian mother was an unfit parent. The court held that although the father claimed the daughter had been substantially affected by the mother's lesbian relationship with another woman, he could point to no evidence in support of his claim. "Our own examination of the record," the court held, "did not uncover any evidence that the daughter was being exposed to deviant sexual acts or that her welfare was being adversely affected in any substantial way."

The wishes of the child are often a factor in custody cases. "Our court has given little significance to the wishes of a six year old child," the Supreme Court held in *Poliakoff v. Poliakoff*. But it has given great weight to the wishes of a child sixteen years of age. See *Guinan v. Guinan*. It is clear that the wishes of a child of any age may be considered, but the weight given to those wishes is governed by the welfare of the children. The judge may interview the child in her chambers if she thinks it will be helpful. Judges usually ask the GAL, lawyer and court reporter to be present.

Children are generally not allowed to testify in Family Court. Rule 23 of the Rules of Family Court reads as follows:

> Generally, in actions of parents against each other, or where the conduct of either parent is an issue, the children should not be allowed in the courtroom during the taking of testimony. Children should not be offered as witnesses as to the misconduct of either parent, except, when, in the discretion of the court, it is essential to establish the facts alleged.

As in so many matters under South Carolina domestic law, fault is not supposed to play a role in the determination of the custody issue; but as a practical matter, it can. Take the most common types of custody cases: one of the spouses, particularly the wife, has committed adultery and the other spouse, usually the husband, is angry, upset and sometimes vindictive. The Supreme Court held many years ago in *Davenport v. Davenport* that consideration of a parent's morality is "limited in its force and effect to what relevancy it has, either directly or indirectly, to the welfare of a child." Numerous cases have upheld this principle ever since. Nevertheless, even though adultery alone is not a reason to take custody from a mother, the courts have said the morality of a parent is a factor to be considered in determining custody. Thus, in an individual case, this may very well be the deciding factor.

Immorality is in the eyes of the beholder. However, our courts want to know what kind of parent each party is. For example, in *Clear v. Clear*, the Court of Appeals made it clear that a good mother who was the child's primary caretaker would not be punished for earning her living as a topless dancer. There was no evidence that her occupation adversely affected her ability to parent the children. Yet in another case, the court held that a father who ran a pornography business was not suitable to have custody of the children.

Courts obviously consider

- domestic violence and sexual abuse;
- the resources of each parent;
- sensitivity to a child's ethnic heritage;
- the education and parenting skills of each parent;
- time available to spend with the child;
- and available help from other family members.

There are many different kinds of custody cases, but by far the most common is when the parents are extremely angry with each other, usually where one spouse has committed adultery and the other spouse seeks to limit the offending parent's access to the children. **These cases are frequently more about the emotions of the parents than they are the welfare of the children.** The wronged spouse usually has strong feelings that while he or she is losing a spouse, they will not lose their children; that the spouse is unfit because he or she committed adultery (which may be the case); that the spouse is going to marry the boyfriend or girlfriend and subject the children to an unhealthy relationship (which it may prove to be); that the spouse is going to leave the state and take the children away; or that the spouse is going to alienate the children and "give the children a new father or mother" (which sometimes happens). These cases make for extremely bitter and expensive custody cases.

Relocation

The other common custody case involves relocation. When the parties separate, one of the parties may want to "go home to mama" or return to his or her family; move back to wherever the couple originally came from; or move to another location so that he or she can have the support of family, friends or a job. These cases are especially difficult because not only are the parties separating, but the separation may mean one parent's total estrangement, as a practical matter, from the children.

South Carolina has recently done a 180-degree turn on the issue of relocation, or whether a custodial parent can leave the state with the children. For many years, South Carolina law discouraged parents from relocating. In 2004, the Supreme Court changed the law in *Latimer v. Farmer* by holding that a father who had custody of a child could relocate without going back to court. The noncustodial parent (in this case, the mother) did not even have the right to go back to Family Court on a claim of changed circumstances and seek custody.

Justice Burnett acknowledged that relocation was "one of the most challenging problems our Family Courts encounter," pitting the custodial parent's freedom to move against the noncustodial parent's right to continue his or her relationship with the child as established before the move. The Supreme Court held that restrictions on relocation "have become antiquated in our increasingly transient society," that the state of the law was confusing and it ought to be clear and that the best interest of the child should trump all other considerations. Remarriage is not a change of circumstance, the court held, and likewise a change of residence of the custodial parent is not a substantial change of circumstance either.

In essence, the custodial parent can move and relocation, standing alone, is not a substantial change of circumstance authorizing the Family Court to change custody. However, the Supreme Court left the door open to litigants in cases when the noncustodial parent can prove that the custodial parent is relocating to spite the other parent or alienate the child from the other parent;

where future contact by the noncustodial parent would be severely restricted or unduly affected and visitation must be realistic enough to "adequately foster an ongoing relationship." Relocation must be of some advantage to the custodial parent and child (i.e., a better job, nearer to family). In the *Latimer* case, the father moved to Michigan and the court made a special provision for live video teleconferences.

In point of fact, no rule on relocation is a fair rule. Some parents simply have to move. Of course, an agreement to stay and not relocate may have changed the result. And the mother in the *Latimer* case had committed adultery. While the courts keep insisting that fault is not a factor in these cases, it is an important wild card in many cases nonetheless.

Another kind of custody case is one in which a parent feels strongly that the other parent is incompetent or unfit, or at least much less competent and much less fit than he or she. Typically these are cases in which one or both of the parties have a mental health, substance abuse or alcohol problem. As difficult as these cases are, they can many times be worked out to where the spouse with the substance abuse problem or mental illness gets treatment and acknowledges his or her problem.

Yet another reason for custody battles is money. The Child Support Guidelines provide that, when the parents have shared custody or joint custody with a significant amount of time for the secondary custodial parent, the guidelines may be modified or may not even apply. The Child Support Guidelines state that if one parent has the child more than 109 overnights, the child support is reduced. Some fathers try to get more time with their children to avoid paying the amount of child support they would otherwise have to pay.

There are many other situations that involve custody litigation. Among younger couples, shared parenting is frequently a fact of life, not a politically correct fantasy. Whereas men until the 1960s and 1970s played a secondary role in the raising of children, that is no longer true today. Therefore, many men, particularly younger men, perceive joint custody as the natural thing to do, as opposed to something "exceptional." Their vision of society, however, is not shared by the Supreme Court of South Carolina, and therein lie the seeds of much discord in divorce cases.

Third Party Rights to Visitation

Third parties have no right to visit a minor child over the objection of the parents. After divorce, third parties may visit with permission of the parent who has the child at the time, whether the custodial parent or noncustodial parent. Thus, grandparents, aunts, uncles, cousins or friends ordinarily see a child in conjunction with the custody/visitation schedule of their family member or friend.

Grandparents who cannot visit their grandchildren with their child or whose child is dead have limited rights of visitation not only under South Carolina law, but under the United States Constitution. In 2000, the United States Supreme Court decided *Troxel v. Granville*. The high court held that parents of minor children have a constitutional right to raise their children as they see fit, and that states cannot force parents to allow visitation with grandparents or other third parties if the parents believe it is not in the children's best interest. Thus, there are constitutional barriers to the ability of Family Court judges to award grandparents visitation with their grandchildren.

In a nutshell, the argument is that children have to be raised by their parents, and that the state has no right to tell parents that their children must have legally enforced visitation rights with grandparents, aunts, uncles, cousins or indeed friends and neighbors. Therefore, the South Carolina Supreme Court has held that "it would seldom, if ever, be in the best interests of the child to grant visitation rights to the grandparents when their child, the parent, has such rights." The Family Court must look carefully at cases where grandparents seek visitation over the objection of their own child.

S.C. Code §20-7-420 (33) allows the Family Court

> to order periods of visitation for the grandparents of a minor child where either...parents of the minor child is...deceased...

and upon a written finding that the visitation rights would be in the best interests of the child and would not interfere with the parent/child relationship. In determining whether to order visitation for the grandparents, the court shall consider the nature of the relationship between the child and the grandparents prior to the filing of the petition or complaint.

In *Camburn v. Smith*, the Supreme Court held that parents and grandparents were not on an equal footing in a contest over visitation. Grandparents must show that the visitation is in the best interests of the child, that it will not interfere with the parent/child relationship and that, given the relationship between grandparents and the grandchildren, there are "compelling circumstances" that overcome the presumption that parental discretion is in the child's best interest if the parent objects to visitation.

These are just some of the scenarios that crop up in custody cases, but the psychological dimensions certainly take precedence over legal theory. This is why people should attempt at all costs to avoid a contested custody case.

The best way to avoid a custody case is to enter into mediation and work out what is now typically called a "parenting plan." The courts, lawyers and counselors would like to see people get away from the idea of custody—in which one party has custody and the other does not—and embrace the idea of a "parenting plan," whereby the parents share time with the children without giving credence to the idea that one party is the "owner" of the children and the other parent is just able to "borrow" them for a short time.

Unfortunately, there is a disconnect between what lawyers, mediators and counselors think is in the best interest of the children and what the law is. Therefore, many hours are spent in mediation and negotiation trying to come up with complicated formulas for visitation, nearly fifty-fifty divisions of time or other ideas that are current throughout our contemporary society when in fact, if the parties litigated the matter, a judge could very well impose the old-fashioned every other weekend visitation plan.

Custody and Visitation

All sorts of common sense terms can also be put into custody agreements to avoid problems in the future, such as

- informing the other party when one party moves or changes his or her address and telephone number;
- forbidding one partner from alienating children from the other parent or allowing others to do so;
- providing for telephone and e-mail visitation;
- providing written notice before either party moves out of state so that the other party can take whatever legal action he or she deems necessary;
- providing that the primary parent or custodial parent shall consult the secondary or the noncustodial parent about important matters in the children's lives, such as educational decisions and non-emergency or major medical treatment.

Obviously, these are matters of simple human decency and courtesy, but people get divorced for a reason.

It is critical in negotiating these agreements, no matter how laborious and time-consuming they may be, that people's major concerns be addressed. Unfortunately, many mediators and lawyers are in such a rush to end the case and "resolve" or "end" the matter that they neglect to include provisions in agreements that are sometimes critical. Litigants need to think through how they feel about having the children for Christmas and not having the children for Christmas. They need to think through their preferences of holidays, pediatricians and the religious upbringing of the child, the schools the children will attend and many other important matters.

On a final note, some parents want to terminate the parental rights of the other parent. This rarely occurs. Indeed, it can only occur where a parent abandons a child, refuses to pay child support or visit for six months, is a danger to the child or has a condition (such as drug addiction or mental illness not likely to change). The courts will only terminate parental rights in these specific cases, and the process is rightly cumbersome and designed to protect parents' right at every stage. See §20-7-1560 to 20-7-1582 S.C. Code.

Chapter 6

Child Support

Ask your child what he wants for dinner only if he's buying.
— Fran Lebowitz

A successful parent is one who raises a child who grows up and is able to pay for her or his own psychoanalysis.
— Nora Ephron

Every parent owes a duty of support to his or her minor child, that is, an unemancipated child under eighteen years of age, unless that child is less than twenty years of age and still in high school, or the child is disabled. As mothers almost always had custody in the past, there are numerous cases and statutes requiring fathers to support their children, which are now equally applicable to mothers who are noncustodial parents.

As a practical matter, child support is almost always established in the divorce action based on the Child Support Guidelines adopted by the state or agreed to by the parties in settling the divorce, property and support issues. Child support usually becomes a contested issue when custody or the extent of visitation also is contested. Contested child support cases can also involve a dispute over the true income of a parent, where one parent earns his income in cash or when one parent or the other is not earning what he or she should. When men are angry, they frequently complain that their ex-wives will not spend the child support on the children. The courts pay absolutely no attention to this allegation unless the father can prove the children are actually neglected.

Child Support Guidelines

The General Assembly enacted a law in 1989 that changed the way child support was addressed in divorce cases. The current law provides that Child Support Guidelines must be applied by the courts in determining the amount of child support for a dependent child, in Section 43-5-480(b) and 20-7-852(a), South Carolina Code of Laws. The guidelines are based on the Income Shares Model, developed by the National Center for State Courts. The model is based on the concept that the children should receive the same proportion of parental income that they would have received had their parents lived together. The model calculates child support as the share of each parent's income that would have been spent on the children if the parents and children were living in the same household. The guidelines are based on the amount of money ordinarily spent on children by their families living in the United States and adjusted to South Carolina cost of living levels.

Expenditures for children in the guidelines include the following nine categories:

- food at home;
- food away from home;
- shelter;
- utilities;
- household goods (furniture, appliances, linens, floor coverings and housewares);
- clothing;
- transportation (other than visitation related);
- ordinary health care;
- and recreation.

Excluded from these expenditure categories are estimated expenditures for child care and extraordinary medical expenses, which have been subtracted because they are added to child support on an as-paid basis. Also excluded from these estimates are personal insurance (e.g. life, disability), gifts, contributions and savings. Because mortgage

Child Support

 The Guidelines are based on the concept that **children should receive the same proportion of parental income** they would have received **had their parents lived together.**

principles are considered to be savings, they are not included in the estimates of child-rearing expenditures.

The guidelines and the accompanying worksheets (which can be found at www.state.sc.us/dss/csed/forms/2006guidelines.pdf) assume that the custodial parent is spending his or her share directly on the child. For the noncustodial parent, the calculated amount establishes the level of child support to be given to the custodial parent for support of the child. See www.state.sc.us/dss/csed for answers to commonly asked questions and a child support calculator; www.divorcehq.com/calculators/sc_supportcalcs.html will take you directly to the calculator.

The guidelines are used for temporary and permanent orders, actions for separate maintenance and support, divorce and child support awards. The guidelines are used to assess the adequacy of agreements for support. The amount of the award that would result from the application of the guidelines is the amount of the child support to be awarded. However, a different amount may be awarded by the court upon a showing that application of the guidelines is inappropriate.

The guidelines provide for child support for a combined parental gross income of up to $20,000 per month, or $240,000 per year. Where the combined gross income is higher, the Family Court should determine child support awards on a case-by-case basis. In cases where the parents' combined monthly gross income is less than $750, the guidelines provide for a case-by-case determination of child support, which should ordinarily be set at no less than $100 per month. The guidelines encourage that child support always be ordered to establish in the payer's mind the principle of the parent's obligation to pay, as well as lay the basis for increased/decreased orders if income changes in the future.

Typical examples of how the guidelines work include the following: a couple has two children, the father makes $75,000 a year, the mother makes $40,000 and the father pays for the children's health insurance ($200 per month). The mother pays the child-care costs of $75 per week, or $325 per month. The father's child support is $991 per month. Another couple has two children, the father earns $150,000 a year and the mother is a stay-at-home mom. The father pays $200 a month in health insurance. There are no child-care costs. The father's child support is $1,811 per month.

Deviation from the guidelines is the exception to the rule. When the Family Court deviates, it must make written findings that clearly state the nature and extent of the variation from the guidelines. The guidelines do not take into account the economic impact of the following factors that can be possible reasons for deviation:

- educational expenses for the child(ren) or the spouse;
- equitable apportionment of property;
- consumer debts;
- families with more than six children;
- unreimbursed extraordinary medical/dental expenses for the noncustodial or custodial parent;
- mandatory deduction of retirement pensions and union fees;
- child-related unreimbursed extraordinary medical expenses;
- monthly fixed payments imposed by court or operation of law;

- significant available income of the child(ren);
- alimony;
- substantial disparity of income in which the noncustodial parent's income is significantly less than the custodial parent's income, thus making it financially impracticable to pay the amount the guidelines indicate the noncustodial parent should pay. This would include situations where the noncustodial parent is disabled and cannot earn above the minimum subsistence level. The court still has the discretion and the independent duty to determine if the amount is reasonable and in the best interest of the child(ren).

Income

The guidelines define "income" as the gross income of the parent, if employed to full capacity, or potential income if unemployed or underemployed. Gross income is used in order to avoid contention over issues of deductibility that would otherwise arise if net income were used. The guidelines are based on the assumption that the noncustodial parent will have only one federal exemption and will have higher taxes than the custodial parent. Adjustments have been made for lower child support payments.

Gross income includes income from any source, including salaries, wages, commissions, royalties, bonuses, rents (less allowable business expenses), dividends, severance pay, pensions, interest, trust income, annuities, capital gains, Social Security benefits (but not Supplemental Social Security Income), workers' compensation benefits, unemployment insurance benefits, veterans' benefits and alimony, including alimony received as a result of another marriage and alimony that a party receives as a result of the current litigation. Unreported income should also be included, if it can be identified.

The court may also take into account assets that are available to generate income for child support. For example, the court may determine the reasonable earning potential of any asset at its market value and assess against it the current treasury bill interest rate, or some other similar appropriate method of computing income.

In addition to determining potential earnings, the court should impute income to any non-income producing assets of either parent, if significant, other than a primary residence or personal property. Examples of such assets are vacation homes (if not maintained as rental property) and idle land.

Gross income does *not* include benefits received from means-tested public assistance programs; income derived by other household members; and/or in-kind income. However, the court should count as income expense reimbursements or in-kind payments received by a parent from self-employment or operation of a business if they are significant and reduce personal living expenses, such as a company car, free housing or reimbursed meals.

For income from self-employment, proprietorship of a business or ownership, a partnership or closely held corporation, gross income is defined as gross receipts minus ordinary and necessary expenses required for self-employment or business operation, including employer's share of FICA. The court should exclude from those expenses amounts allowed by the Internal Revenue Service for accelerated depreciation of investment tax credits for purposes of the guidelines and add those amounts back in to determine gross income. In general, the courts carefully review income and expenses from self-employment or operation of a business to determine actual levels of gross income available to the parent to satisfy a child support obligation. As may be apparent, this amount may differ from the determination of business income for tax purposes.

If the Family Court finds that a parent is voluntarily unemployed or underemployed, it should calculate child support based on a determination of the potential income that would ordinarily be available to the parent. If income is imputed to a custodial parent, the court may also impute reasonable day care expenses. However, the court may take into account the presence of young children or handicapped children who must be cared for by the parent, necessitating the parent's inability to work. The court may also factor in considerations of rehabilitative alimony in order to enable the parent to become employed.

In order to impute income to a parent who is unemployed or underemployed, the court should determine the employment potential and probable earnings level of the parent based on that parent's recent work history, occupational qualifications and prevailing job opportunities and earning levels in the community. Potential income of parents unemployed or underemployed is difficult to establish, and the courts try to balance the needs of the child and a parent's actual ability to pay. For example, a lawyer can quit his job and work for indigent clients, but his regular income would be imputed. Voluntary underemployment can result in court imputing income to a father, but a father who did not earn as much as he could have during the marriage apparently need not work harder or even up to his true capacity after the divorce (see *Arnal v. Arnal*). The Supreme Court held recently that bad faith was not required where the father was underemployed.

Ordinarily, the court will determine income from the financial declarations filed with the court. However, in the absence of a financial declaration, or where the amount reflected on the financial declaration may be an issue, the court may rely on suitable documentation of current earnings, preferably using such documents as pay stubs, employer statements or receipts and expenses if the parent is self-employed.

An award of alimony should be taken into consideration when utilizing the guidelines as a deduction from the payer spouse's gross income, and as gross income received by the recipient spouse. Lump sum, rehabilitative reimbursement or any other alimony may be considered by the court as a reason for deviation from the guidelines.

Any previous or existing court orders requiring the payment of child support, alimony or both should be protected by any subsequent child support order. Alimony actually paid as a result of another marriage or child support actually paid for the benefit of children other than those considered in the computation, to the extent such payment or payments are required by a previous or existing court order, should be deducted from gross income.

Either parent receives credit for additional natural or adopted children living in the home, but not for stepchildren, unless a court order establishes a legal responsibility. Such credit will be given whether or not such children are supported by a third party. This recognizes the custodial parent's responsibility and share in supporting those other children in the home, just like that parent's responsibility and share to the child or children in the present calculation.

Health Insurance

The Family Court will consider provisions for adequate health insurance coverage for children in every child support order. Ordinarily, the court should require coverage by that parent who can obtain the most comprehensive coverage through an employer or otherwise, at the most reasonable cost. If either parent carries health insurance for the child(ren) who is to receive support, the cost of the coverage should be added. If the employer provides some measure of the coverage, only that amount actually paid by the employee should be added. The portion of the health insurance premium that covers the children is the only expense that should be added. If this amount cannot be verified, the total cost of the premium should be divided by the total number of persons covered by the policy and then multiplied by the number of children in the support order.

Whichever party is responsible for paying the health insurance premium will receive a credit. The guidelines are based on the assumption that the custodial parent will be responsible for up to $250 per year per child in uninsured medical expenses. Extraordinary medical expenses, not addressed in the guidelines, are defined as reasonable and necessary uninsured medical expenses in excess of $250 per year per child. Under this definition, what is "reasonable and necessary"—e.g. orthodontia and professional counseling— would be at the discretion of the court. Extraordinary unreimbursed medical expenses addressed by the court shall be divided into pro rated percentages based on the proportional share of combined monthly gross income.

The cost of day care the parent incurs due to employment or the search for employment, net of the federal income tax credit for such day care, is to be added to the basic obligation. This is to encourage parents to work and generate income for themselves as well as their children. However, day care costs must be reasonable, not to exceed the level required to provide high-quality care for children from a licensed provider. As custodial parents may be eligible for qualified tax credits, the actual day care expense should be adjusted to recognize this credit.

Expenditures on children increase during teenage years. Expenditures on children in the twelve to seventeen age group are significantly higher than expenditures on children in the infant to eleven age group. Given that child rearing expenditures are higher for older children, an issue in the development of the guidelines was whether there should be age adjustments; that is, whether the guidelines should incorporate separate scales by age of the children. However, since the guidelines are based on economic data that represents estimates of total expenditures on child rearing up to age eighteen, except for child care and most health care costs, the need for separate scales was eliminated.

The Family Court can determine a total child support obligation by adding the basic child support obligation, health insurance premium (portion covering children) and work-related child care costs.

The total child support obligation is divided between the parents in proportion to their income. Each parent's proportional share of combined adjusted gross income must be calculated. One may compute the obligation of each parent by multiplying each parent's share of income by the total child support obligation, and give the necessary credit for adjustments to the basic combined child support obligation.

Although a monetary obligation is computed for each parent, the guidelines presume that the custodial parent will spend that parent's share directly on the child in that parent's custody. In cases of joint custody or split custody, where both parents have responsibility of the child for a substantial portion of the time, there are provisions for adjustments.

Custodial Arrangements

Contrary to the law of the state as announced by the Supreme Court, the guidelines state, "When both parents are deemed fit, and other relevant logistical circumstances apply, shared custody should be encouraged in order to ensure the maximum involvement by both parents in the life of the child." The guidelines go on to state that "the shared custody adjustment, however, is advisory and not compulsory. The court should consider each case individually before applying the adjustment to ensure that it does not produce a substantial negative effect on the child(ren)'s standard of living."

For purposes of the guidelines, shared physical custody means that each parent has court-ordered visitation with the children overnight for more than 109 overnights each year (30 percent), and that both parents contribute to the expenses of the child(ren) in addition to the payment of child support. If a parent with visitation does not exercise the visitation as ordered by the Family Court, the custodial parent may petition the court for a reversion to the level of support calculated under the guidelines without the shared parenting adjustment. The shared physical custody adjustment is an annual adjustment only and should not be used when the proportion of overnights exceeds 30 percent for a shorter period, e.g., a month. For example, child support is not abated during a month-long summer visitation. This adjustment should be applied without regard to legal custody of the child(ren). Legal custody refers to decision-making authority with respect to the child(ren). If the 109 overnights threshold is reached for shared physical custody, this adjustment may be applied even if one parent has sole legal custody.

Child support cases with shared physical custody are calculated using a different worksheet than that used for traditional custody cases; this worksheet has its own formula designed to lessen the child support obligation of the party with less physical custody.

Split custody refers to the custody arrangements where there are two or more children and each parent has physical custody of at least one child. Using the guidelines, the Family Court should determine a theoretical support payment for the child or children in the custody of the other. The obligation is then offset, with the parent owing the larger amount paying the next amount to the other parent. In split custody arrangements, the guidelines arrive at separate computations for the child or children residing with each parent. The support obligation must then be prorated among all children in the household. For example, if there are three children due support, with two residing with one parent and one with the other, the court should calculate support amounts using the table for three children, with one-third of that amount being used to determine the basic child support obligation for one child and two-thirds for the other two children.

College Expenses

Child support ends normally when a child graduates from high school, or is working and is over eighteen years of age. But there can be special circumstances where support can be ordered for adult children over the age of eighteen. One special circumstance is contributing to the college education of an adult child. A Family Court judge can require a parent to contribute that amount of money necessary to enable a child over eighteen to attend high school and four years of college, where there is evidence that:

- the characteristics of the child indicate that he or she will benefit from college;
- the child demonstrates the ability to do well, or at least make satisfactory grades;
- the child cannot otherwise go to school;
- the parent has the financial ability to help pay for such an education.

The court should also consider the availability of loans and grants to the student and the ability of the child to earn income during the school year and on vacation. It is unclear whether children in college have a duty to minimize their expenses. Many cases arise over issues of spending money, travel and medical expenses.

Once again, draftsmanship of an agreement is critical. Where an agreement requires a parent to pay "all college expenses," the court will strictly enforce it even if the parent cannot afford to pay the expenses. This is because a court cannot vary the terms of an unambiguous contract. Sometimes it is better to leave the terms of who will pay for college vague—as in, "Each party will be bound by the law of the State of South Carolina as to their contribution, if any to the college expenses of the children," or more specifically, "Each parent will contribute a pro-rata share of his or her income to the reasonable and necessary college expenses (tuition, room and board, and books) of the children at a state-supported institution of higher learning in the state of South Carolina." Some parties set aside specific funds for the college educations of the children. Many families now have 529 savings accounts (see www.saveforcollege.com for example) or accounts they themselves set aside for the college education of the children.

It should be noted that the issue of college expenses only arises when a child is ready to go to college. The Family Court cannot order a parent to save for college or set aside money to do so. But it is important to address the issue in the final agreement, as some states do not require parents to contribute to the college expenses of a child, and if one or both parties move from South Carolina, the payment of college expenses may not be required of a parent.

Parents may also be liable for the support of a child over the age of eighteen "where there are physical or mental disabilities of the child" that warrant support. Even after a child has become emancipated, parents may still be liable for severely injured or retarded adult children. A parent can be ordered to pay for expensive therapeutic boarding schools if they are deemed necessary to the health of a child.

Chapter 7

Lawyer's Fees and Costs

Marriage is really tough because you have to deal with feelings and lawyers.

—Richard Pryor

A man may as well open an oyster without a knife as a lawyer's mouth without a fee.

—Barten Holyday (1618)

When I started practicing law in the 1970s, the statute on legal fees and the cases actually called women "privileged suitors." The law was clear that, given the fact that women were dependent, there was no way they could afford to retain an attorney. In order for women to be able to present their case, the Family Court had to award fees so that wives could secure a lawyer. Modern life has changed the law. Women are no longer "privileged suitors" because our law is now gender neutral. The dependent spouse—whether a husband or a wife—if not exactly a "privileged suitor," is still entitled to legal fees in order to present his or her case in court.

South Carolina law provides that the Family Court may, from time to time, considering the financial resources and marital fault of both parties, order one party to pay a reasonable amount to the other for attorney fees, expert fees, investigation fees, costs and suit money in divorce cases, as well as in actions for separate maintenance and support. These include fees and costs incurred before the commencement for the proceeding and after the entry of judgment, *pendente lite* and permanently. See §20-3-130(H) S.C. Code.

Need for Retainer

Family Court judges are well aware of the economics of divorce. Most Family Court judges practiced family law at some point and know that many spouses are able to afford a competent attorney, but a dependent housewife or disabled husband with no income or readily available assets cannot do so. Judges are also aware that the spouse who earns the money and controls the assets (the "moneyed side of the case," in lawyer jargon) can starve the dependent spouse out and force him or her into a situation where they have to compromise on both temporary issues and in a final settlement, unless the Family Court levels the playing field by making an award of attorney's fees and costs to the dependent spouse.

Parties need attorney's fees at the beginning of the case more than they do at the end of the case. Most lawyers will not take on a complicated or contested custody or divorce case without being paid a retainer in advance. The amount of the retainer varies from lawyer to lawyer, as does the hourly rate. Hourly rates vary in this state from $100 per hour to $600 per hour. Retainers range from $500 to tens of thousands of dollars, depending on the attorney and the complexity of the case. Of course, neither party may need the aid of the court in securing attorney's fees if they both have the resources to pay their own lawyers. (Anyone contemplating a divorce ought to make financial arrangements in advance to pay fees and costs.) Many parties have their own bank accounts and assets, and therefore can pay their own attorneys at the beginning of the case and make a claim against the other party for reimbursement of those fees at the end of the case.

However, one spouse usually has greater access to funds to pay lawyers than the other spouse. In the traditional scenario, the wife has a number of choices. First, she can secretly save money to pay fees.

Second, she can borrow funds from family or friends. Third, she can withdraw funds from joint accounts or other marital funds or obtain an advance on a joint credit card. I have been involved in numerous cases where temporary control of money and the ability to borrow money, mortgage property, use an existing line of credit or charge on credit cards has been a critical factor at the commencement of litigation. It is always wise for both spouses to know where the assets are, how they are titled, how one can gain access to these funds, whether or not credit cards can be charged against and whether or not funds can be removed from one account to another account.

In this world of electronic banking, accounts one thinks are inaccessible sometimes are just the opposite. My favorite story in this regard involved a client whose husband would not leave the marital home, even though he told his wife he wanted a divorce. He wanted to drive her out with no money. I could not convince her husband or his attorney or a Family Court judge to eject the husband from the home because there was no legally sufficient basis to do so. The wife and I then hit on the idea that she could remove all of the money in the parties' joint account and put it into an account solely in her name. She literally wrote a check on an out-of-state bank for $1 million and had the funds wired to her own separate account. It was truly amazing to see how quickly the legal system worked once the wife had the husband's $1 million under her control! The husband moved out the day he found out. The court issued various orders. And needless to say, the wife had no problem paying legal fees.

It is also possible for a dependent spouse to borrow money on marital assets. I have had a number of cases where the marital home was titled solely in the wife's name, usually because the husband wanted to protect himself from creditors, not realizing that a wife might also be a major creditor. In these instances, the wife is able—with the help of friendly bankers—to borrow substantial money by mortgaging the house and taking out an equity loan to pay for legal fees and her other expenses.

When parties are living together, both parties have the legal right to all funds that they can legally obtain, meaning if the bank account is jointly titled or if it allows access by the wife, she can legally move the funds. The husband's reaction, however, must be taken into account. The Family Court is well aware that wives move money from joint accounts or charge legal fees on credit cards, and while the husband is often irate, this procedure does allow the wife to obtain counsel of her choice at a time when she may need counsel to act immediately. The Family Court judges generally understand that "taking money" or charging fees on credit cards is sometimes necessary, so long as the money is not dissipated and is properly accounted for. The court also knows that there will be an accounting at the end of the case and, while the wife may have temporary use of the funds, in the end, the court can balance the equities and require the wife to pay her own attorney's fees or, if it is appropriate, order the husband to do so at a final hearing.

The cost of the litigation is a key component in the overall settlement. If lawyers worked for free, clients would readily go to trial to see if they could get a better result or obtain more property or money. But because legal fees are part of the equation, litigants have to figure in the cost of the litigation versus the benefit to be obtained. This cost/benefit ratio is something that every client should discuss openly with his or her attorney. Unfortunately, one has to put a price tag on how much custody and visitation one really wants, or whether the offer on the table with regard to alimony and property division is sufficient. This should be a business decision. Of course, in matters involving the health, safety and welfare of children, other considerations come into play.

The issue of temporary legal fees frequently takes on a much bigger role in the litigation than it should. Some husbands are outraged that their wives retain lawyers and "waste" their hard-earned money on legal fees designed to extract still more money from them. Legal fees paid by the dependent spouse from marital funds will sometimes infuriate the other spouse more than any other issue in the case. But in the end, both parties will have to incur whatever fees and costs are necessary in order to resolve the litigation, and the fees should be seen as a necessary part of the cost of dissolving the marital partnership.

Most parties settle their cases. The issue of attorney's fees, especially the wife's (or the dependent husband's) attorney's fees, frequently remains an emotionally charged issue in the settlement negotiations and in mediation. It should not be, because both parties are in need of legal advice.

In those rare instances where there is a trial, or in those more frequent instances where litigants go to court on matters of temporary support, custody or use of the home, the Family Court may award attorney's fees to one party to be paid by the other party. Family Court judges generally decline to award legal fees when both parties can afford to pay their own lawyers, unless one party's behavior has been particularly unreasonable. Where the parties' financial situation is not equal, judges generally award fees to the prevailing party. Of all the factors set forth in the law, the results obtained by one party against the other are the most important factor. Where the court is convinced that the party seeking fees had no other choice but to bring the matter to the court and the other party was found to be wrong, it is only fair that the prevailing party be awarded fees.

In determining whether to award attorney's fees, the court should consider each party's ability to pay his or her own fees; the beneficial

results obtained by the attorney; the parties' respective financial conditions; and the effect of the fee on each party's standard of living. See *E.D.M. v. T.A.M* and *Doe v. Doe*. In determining the amount of attorney's fees to award, the court should consider the nature, extent and difficulty of the services rendered; the time necessarily devoted to the case; the professional standing of counsel; the contingency of compensation; the beneficial results obtained; and the customary legal fees for similar services. See *Griffith v. Griffith*.

If a party is not the primary prevailing party or prevails only partially, the factor of beneficial results accomplished will weigh in favor of reducing the fee, as the time and labor devoted to the issues lost should not be charged against the opposing party who prevailed on those issues.

Many litigants, particularly women whose husbands have left them, feel that they should not have to pay legal fees at all. As L.J. Bowen noted, "There is one panacea which heals every sore in litigation, and that is costs." In the opinion of these litigants, the erring husband should pay all fees from day one. Family Court judges frequently agree, but not always. Family law attorneys make their living representing clients on an hourly basis. Therein lies the rub. A client without access to funds still must pay her lawyer a retainer. The answer to the problem is planning ahead and obtaining sufficient funds for a retainer against which the lawyer can bill.

At a temporary hearing, the Family Court can order the "moneyed spouse" (traditionally the husband) to advance to the "unmoneyed spouse" (traditionally the wife) sufficient funds to pay fees through a trial. Frequently, attorneys for the husband agree to advance a lump sum to the wife as an advance on her equitable apportionment award and leave the issue of who pays the lawyers until the end of the case. This saves a lot of bickering about legal fees, which, of course, neither husband nor wife wants to pay. It is usually in the husband's interest to advance funds, because temporary hearings can be expensive and time-consuming and most judges will see to it that the wife has access to a lawyer.

Legal fees are one of the most emotional components of a settlement. Many spouses loudly oppose paying their other spouse's lawyer. Talking one spouse into paying his or her spouse's legal fees is an unpalatable task for any lawyer. In the end, however, the fees and the costs (private investigators, court reporters, process servers, CPAs, other experts) have to be paid, and it can be stated explicitly in the settlement agreement or the money to pay fees can be embedded in the value of assets the wife is to receive; thus, if there is a dispute about the value of real estate, a company, collectibles or any asset, money to pay the dependent spouse's attorneys fees can be transferred by assigning higher values so that he or she gets the funds and the angry payor spouse saves face.

Unfortunately, legal fees can and often do play a major role in the outcome of a divorce case, just as access to lawyers and the money to pay them can and does affect all litigation. Lawyers are prohibited from representing clients in marital litigation on a contingency fee basis. The reasoning behind this is the fear that lawyers would have a vested interest in the case going forward in order to collect fees, whereas public policy favors reconciliation. Whatever the reasoning, lawyers can only bill by the hour, except in suits for arrears (money owed) on account of unpaid alimony or child support. Thus, in marital litigation both parties must be able to pay their separate attorneys. Lawyers are also prohibited from representing both parties in drafting an agreement because there would be a conflict of interest.

Unfortunately, **legal fees can and often do play a major role in the outcome of a divorce case**, just as access to lawyers and the money to pay them can and does affect all litigation.

The court can and does consider the misconduct of a litigant in prolonging the resolution of the case. The Court of Appeals held in *Taylor v. Taylor,*

> In the case at hand, the evidence shows Husband has brought the Family Court against Wife and appealed all three...Wife has consistently prevailed on most of the issues, yet this has not tempered Husband's propensity to haul Wife back into court time and time again. Husband is clearly in a financial position to handle these suits, while Wife is not. We further have the added dimension of an uncooperative husband who did much to prolong and hamper a final resolution of the issues in this case. An adversary spouse should not be rewarded for such conduct.

Chapter 8

Agreements

Agree, for the law is costly.

—Thomas Fuller (1732)

Lawsuit, *n*. a machine which you go into as a pig and come out as a sausage.

—Ambrose Bierce, *The Devil's Dictionary*

There are several different types of agreements related to marriage and divorce: premarital (or ante-nuptial) agreements; post-nuptial and/or reconciliation agreements; separation agreements; and final custody, support and property settlement agreements.

Nuptial Agreements

We are all familiar with ante-nuptial and premarital agreements. In the old days, the very wealthy Hollywood actors made prenuptial agreements famous. The law disfavored prenuptial agreements for a long time for the obvious reason that a wealthy husband could avoid his obligations to his wife at the time of divorce. However, the Supreme Court of South Carolina has held since the early 1980s that premarital agreements do not violate public policy, "but are highly beneficial to serving the best interest of the marital relationship." Nevertheless, premarital agreements cannot affect the obligations of the parties to one another while they are married. This would violate public policy.

Agreements

In *Towles v. Towles*, the Supreme Court held that a wife who agreed not to sue her husband in order to reconcile with him would not be held to that agreement, as it was against public policy. The court held that an agreement not to sue is tantamount to a release of the husband of his duty to perform his essential marital obligations, and it is therefore void as against public policy. In recent years, however, the court has been more willing to enforce prenuptial agreements.

The General Assembly gave parties the ability to exclude property by means of a contract. The Equitable Apportionment Act allows for parties to make any property nonmarital property by entering into a written contract, including prenuptial agreements between the parties "which must be considered presumptively fair and equitable so long as it was voluntarily executed with both parties separately represented by counsel and pursuant to the full financial disclosure to each other that is mandated by the rules of the Family Court as to income, debts and assets." In other words, the General Assembly has provided that there is a presumption that a premarital agreement is fair so long as both parties are represented by separate (and preferably) competent counsel and there is full financial disclosure on the financial declaration form required by the Family Court.

In *Hardee v. Hardee*, the Supreme Court of South Carolina affirmed the validity of a prenuptial agreement where the wife was in ill health and the husband was having an affair with another woman. The Family Court found that a waiver of alimony, support and attorney's fees was void as unconscionable. The Supreme Court reversed and held that the courts have reconsidered public policy in light of societal changes and that today premarital agreements, so long as they do not promote divorce or otherwise offend public policy, are favored. The court pointed out that prenuptial agreements cannot be enforced if they were obtained through fraud, duress or mistake; misrepresentation or non-disclosure of material facts; if the agreement was unconscionable; and if the facts and circumstances have changed since the agreement was executed so as to make its enforcement unfair or unreasonable. Even though the wife in *Hardee* was disabled, the court held that she had serious health problems at the time of the signing of the agreement and the premarital agreement specifically noted her health problems, all of which were foreseeable.

Separation agreements involve agreements between the parties when they are separated and after marriage. These agreements have been discussed above.

Post-nuptial or reconciliation agreements are agreements entered into in contemplation of resuming the marital relationship. As South Carolina's public policy favors reconciliation, it is likely that our Supreme Court would uphold reconciliation agreements, although there is no case on this point as yet.

Property Settlement Agreements

Property settlement, support and custody agreements are like any other contract, except that the agreement must be approved for fairness by the Family Court. Negotiating a contract in a divorce case involves the same considerations inherent in all contracts. If you settle a divorce case and neglect to address important issues, like any other party to a contract, you suffer the consequences. Whether you are represented by an attorney or not, a person entering into a contract is presumed to have read and understood it. Claiming later that you never read the contract is no more a defense in Family Court than it is in any other court. If you forget to include a provision about life insurance or health insurance, you have lost your right to claim it. You cannot come back and renegotiate the contract later. It is final and binding as to every matter in it, except matters relating to custody and visitation of children and child support, which are always subject to review by a court if there is a substantial change of circumstance.

The purpose of an agreement is to end all controversy between the parties. Thus, it is critical that the agreement be written in clear, unambiguous language. The key to a good settlement agreement is the old saying KISS, "Keep It Simple, Stupid." The simpler and clearer the agreement, the fewer problems later. It is also critical that all issues are addressed. Once the decree of divorce or final order approving the agreement is issued, the Family Court loses jurisdiction over all issues between the parties except issues related to children and enforcement of the agreement, unless the agreement provides that the court continue to supervise a specific transaction, such as the sale of the former marital home. If you forgot to ask for alimony or to transfer a particular piece of property, the issue is gone with the wind.

As clarity is the key to an agreement, you should make a detailed list of all your personal property (furniture, books, tools, jewelry) you want out of the former marital home and list each and every bank, money market or stock account. All species of property should be accounted for, or else the title owner gets to keep it. (See the checklist of assets at www.straighttalkscdivorce.com.) An ounce of prevention (identifying everything specifically in the agreement) is worth a pound of cure (litigating the issue later).

Settlement agreements can and should end *all* controversies between the parties, including potential civil suits or claims between the parties or third parties. Family Court does not have jurisdiction of claims for assault and battery, slander, libel, fraud, giving the other spouse a sexually transmitted disease or any other tort or civil claims. But a general release of all claims in the divorce agreement ends all future litigation between the parties. Similarly, releases can include suits or claims against paramours, business partners, business entities, friends or family members for a variety of claims. Ideally the agreement means finality.

Settlement agreements can and **should end all controversies between the parties**, including potential civil suits or claims between the parties or third parties.

Take Care in Drafting Agreements

One of the biggest mistakes people make in divorce cases is not paying enough attention to the details of their agreements. Although settlement and mediation are good, mediators, attorneys and parties all suffer from a tendency to rush into agreements in order to "bring this matter to a close" without spending the time necessary to write a proper agreement that will govern the parties' lives well into the future. The adage "haste makes waste" is particularly appropriate to divorce agreements, where everyone, including the lawyers, is in a rush. The parties are tired of paying legal fees. The lawyers want to get the matter concluded. The mediators want to settle because settling is their mission. The system is set up to rush into agreements and get them signed. This is a tremendous mistake.

An agreement should be read carefully by the parties. The parties should go over their checklists, including the checklists at my website, www.straighttalkscdivorce.com. The agreement should address anything and everything that either party has the least concern about, because once it is signed and approved by the court, it is a contract that cannot be changed. Agreements should address every issue between the parties, including the division of all kinds of property. Clients and lawyers both hate to deal with the issue of the "pots and pans," but it is a simple matter, although it may be time-consuming, to make a list of all the personal property that you want and attach that list to the agreement. The division and transfer of property should be spelled out in detail. If the contract does not clearly give a party a right to property, the property will be lost to that party.

All tax issues should be addressed, including who shall pay the taxes that *both* parties are liable for in the future if the Internal Revenue Service or the South Carolina Tax Commission determines that past tax returns were erroneous. If the parties filed

joint tax returns, both parties remain liable for the taxes regardless of what the agreement says. If one party fails to report income or committed tax fraud, substantial taxes, penalties and interest could be assessed against *both* parties. While the parties cannot prevent the IRS or the Tax Commission from making a claim against them, they can agree that the party at fault will hold the other party harmless and pay all fees and costs incurred by the wronged party. But if this matter is not addressed in the agreement, both parties remain liable for the taxes and penalties and the Family Court can do nothing about it.

All debts should be addressed specifically. Typically, parties have credit card debt, notes, mortgages, automobile payments and other loans. Again, both parties may be liable to a bank or credit card company or other creditors. Again, neither party is released from his or her liability by a settlement agreement in Family Court, which is why it is so important to discover all debts, pay them off if possible from marital property or allocate the debt and provide for a hold harmless. To obtain credit reports, contact the three major credit bureaus:

- Equifax at 1-800-685-1111 or www.equifax.com
- Experian at 1-888-397-3742 or www.experian.com
- TransUnion at 1-800-888-4213 or www.transunion.com

One problem that comes up from time to time is the misuse of forms by lawyers and their staff. Lawyers tend to use forms stored in their computers. Unfortunately, the forms they use may or may not contain clauses *apropos* to the case at hand. The forms may contain clauses that should not be included in the agreement. I have seen agreements that contain the wrong names of the parties or the children because the lawyer's secretary used a "go by" (another client's agreement) and the lawyer failed to proofread it. A computer is a wonderful tool, but *there is no substitute for reading the final contract itself.* As agreements go through different drafts, clauses are deleted or added, and one has to be certain that the version you are signing is the version you think you are signing.

Another common problem is security for payment of funds by one spouse to the other. When parties divide property, it is critical that they actually divide it, i.e., sign deeds, bills of sale, titles to vehicles and transfer accounts quickly. Once the property is gone, it may not be recovered. Some agreements provide that one party will pay the other a sum of money to balance the equities. It is wise to secure these payments by means of a note and mortgage or lien on real estate or securities. This, however, requires a lawyer knowledgeable in preparing such instruments. Many family law attorneys have no idea how to draft notes, mortgages, liens or security instruments, and a real estate or transactional lawyer may be needed to do so. Once again, this is irritating at the end of a case, and more legal fees are incurred. But notice that bankers do not get irritated by having *their* lawyers be certain *their* notes are properly secured by *their* mortgages.

 A computer is a wonderful tool, but **there is no substitute for reading the final contract itself.**

Agreements should be specific as to how property is to be sold. The classic situation is the abandoned wife who is forced to sell the former marital home. Unless an agreement is highly specific as to the real estate agent, the selling price (and how to reduce it), showing the house to prospective purchasers and a time frame for the wife to be out of the house, the husband may be back in court fighting about the sale of the house for years to come. No sales price is high enough when the ex-wife wants to stay in the house; no agent is good enough. This is one reason why it is better to divide property in kind, if possible, rather than sell it.

Agreements should address every issue that was contested or could have been contested:

- custody (with detailed provisions for visitation and restraining orders);
- alimony (whether waived or to be paid, the amount and clear wording as to a beginning and an end);
- child support (including health insurance, life insurance, educational expenses, summer camps, college);
- property division (noting all major items of property, escrow accounts, previously undisclosed debts);
- insurance issues (life, health, disability, property taxes, income taxes);
- legal fees and releases;
- and restraining orders concerning the behavior of the parents while they are with the children (addressing such questions as whether girlfriends and boyfriends are going to be allowed to be around the children).

Court Approval of Agreement

Marital agreements are unique contracts under South Carolina law, as they must be approved by the Family Court. In 1983, the Supreme Court decided in *Moseley v. Mosier*,

The parties may specifically agree that the amount of alimony may not ever be modified by the court; they may contract out of any continuing judicial supervision of their relationship by the court; they may agree that the periodic payments or alimony stated in the decree shall be judicially awarded, enforceable by contempt, but not modifiable by the court; they may agree to any terms they wish as long as the court deems the contract to have been entered fairly, voluntarily and reasonably. With the court's approval, the terms become part of the decree and are binding on the parties and the court. However, unless the agreement unambiguously denies the court jurisdiction, the terms will be modifiable by the court and enforceable by contempt.

Family Court has to approve *all* agreements, including property divisions, custody and child support.

Marital agreements, like all contracts, must be supported by consideration (the giving up and receiving of benefits and losses). They must be voluntary; they must be fair to both parties and to the children; and they must be entered into freely and voluntarily. The judge must hold a hearing and question the parties, evaluate the agreement and review the financial declarations. There is a strong preference that both parties be present in court. Family Court judges ask each party a list of questions:

- Is the agreement fair?
- Did you enter into the agreement freely and voluntarily?
- Are you satisfied with the services of your lawyer?
- Can you do the things you have agreed to do?
- Do you accept the tax consequences of this agreement?
- Have you given and received full financial disclosure?
- Are you under the influence of alcohol, drugs or anything, stress included, which may affect your ability to understand this agreement?

- Do you understand that once the court approves this agreement, it cannot be modified except as to issues involving the child, which are always modifiable?
- Do you wish me to approve this agreement and make it an order of the court subject to the contempt powers of the court?

Marital agreements should be in writing. As Samuel Goldwyn once said, "A verbal contract isn't worth the paper it's written on." But it is possible for the parties to reach a verbal agreement and go to court and put it on the record. The judge can approve such an agreement. And there are cases where the parties reach a verbal agreement, one party relies on it and the court later enforces it. In one such case, a father promised to help pay college expenses for his daughters if the mother stopped a proceeding for an increase in child support. The mother did so, and when the father refused to pay for one half of the college expenses, the Family Court required him to do so. But I would follow Sam Goldwyn's advice anyway.

Fraud vitiates all contracts, but it is extremely difficult to set aside an agreement approved by the Family Court, because each party has the opportunity to discover property, and if one party failed to do it, the courts are reluctant to set an agreement approved by the court—now a judgment of a court—aside.

Chapter 9

After the Divorce

I know a couple that got remarried. He missed two alimony payments and she repossessed him.

— Bill Barner

Every divorced person has homework after the divorce. The first order of business, after seeing to it that all property transfers are made, is to change your will. **A divorce voids a will**. I have had cases where one of the warring parties died and left everything to his soon-to-be former wife, by inadvertence. Changes of names need to be shared with government agencies, especially the Social Security Administration.

What happens after a divorce depends on what happened during the divorce. The more careful and prepared you are in reducing your resolution to an understandable agreement ("KISS"), the fewer problems you should have after the divorce. Once the court approves the agreement or issues a final order in a contested case, the parties are obliged to obey the order and live by their agreement or the final decision of a court. (Of course, if one party appeals from an order of the court, the appeal stays (delays) the division of property, but does not stay orders regarding custody, alimony and child support.)

Property transfers usually cause the least number of problems, unless one of the litigants refuses to sign a deed. The most common problem does not lie with the parties, but with their attorneys. Once the case is over, many lawyers feel that their job is done, and some do not take the details of the divorce as a transaction seriously. But proper deeds have to be drawn; mortgages have to be drafted, satisfied

> Common problems after the divorce include refinancing mortgages, having Qualified Domestic Relations Orders (QDROs) prepared and being sure all joint debts are paid.

and recorded; debts have to be paid; QDROs have to be written to transfer monies in retirement funds; and numerous other details attend finalizing a divorce. Of course, it is up to the parties themselves, not just the lawyers, to see that these transactions take place.

Common problems after the divorce include having the other spouse comply with provisions to refinance the mortgage on the marital home. You do not want to be obligated on a note and mortgage that you have to show as a liability on your financial statement if it is not absolutely necessary. You must follow up with your attorney to have the Qualified Domestic Relations Order (QDRO) issued, or the money in the retirement accounts will not be transferred. It is critical that debts that are supposed to be paid are in fact paid, because one never knows what will happen in the future, and even though an agreement or divorce decree requires one party to pay a credit card debt, it does not mean that party will pay it. Later when they file for bankruptcy or are unable to pay it, the credit card company will be coming after you. Parties cannot take for granted a change in ownership or beneficiary of life insurance policies, the creation of trusts, maintenance of health insurance and myriad other details that can affect one's life. If a business is to be sold or transferred, if stock or memberships in an LLC are to be conveyed, it is wise to see to these matters promptly and to see them through.

Contempt of Court

In extreme situations, where a party will not comply with a court order, the Family Court has the authority to bring that party before the court on a charge of contempt. Family Court orders are just that: orders to do something. Therefore, if a party has been ordered to transfer property, the failure of that party to do so can subject the offending person to contempt of court. Family Court judges have authority to incarcerate people guilty of contempt for up to one year in jail, levy a fine of up to $1,500, order the offending person to perform up to three hundred hours of community service and award attorney's fees. Contempt is an extreme remedy, and the courts hold that in order for a person to be in contempt, the contempt must be willful and the evidence of it must be clear and convincing. If a spouse is unable, without fault of his or her own, to obey the order, he or she should not be held in contempt.

A party may not be found in contempt for the violation of a court order that is subject to interpretation. ("One may not be convicted of contempt for violating a court order which fails to tell him in definite terms what he must do. The language of the commands must be clear and certain rather than implied.") A court may not hold a person in contempt where his conduct could be interpreted as consistent with the court's order. The violation must be deliberate. Mere inadvertence or honest mistake will not constitute contempt. The act must be done willfully and for an illegitimate or improper purpose. "A willful act is defined as one done voluntarily and intentionally with the specific intent to fail to do something the law requires to be done; that is to say with bad purpose either to disobey or disregard the law."

But when someone simply refuses, after being requested, to do what is required of him or her, a Family Court judge will have no problem finding that person in contempt, so long as the terms of the order are clear. When a contempt action is brought, the issue of retroactive modification of support payments that have already accrued is also automatically before the court. The Family Court has the authority to modify a previous decree as to installments of alimony that have already accrued upon a showing of altered circumstances. In making such a modification, the court may consider whether a spouse is unable to pay accrued alimony due to financial reasons or other just cause.

(This is distinguishable from child support payment modifications, which are not effective as to any installment accruing prior to the filing of the action for modification. S.C. Code Ann. Section 20-7-933. The court may, however, hold child support arrearage in abeyance.)

Where a party refuses to obey a court order and may have even left the state, the Family Court has extraordinary power to appoint a sequestrator, i.e., a trustee or receiver who, like any receiver, can take the property in question into his legal possession and cause the title to be issued to the other party by the clerk of court. Thus, assets of a party in violation of an order can be seized by the court and conveyed to the rightful party. See Section 20-7-475 S.C. Code.

More typical is the everyday problem of parents who fail to pay alimony or child support. Most agreements and orders require that if a party is more than five days late in making a payment of alimony or child support, future payments must be made through the clerk of the Family Court, together with the required service charge (currently 5 percent of the court-ordered amount). This is quite onerous, because instead of the parent simply mailing an alimony or child support check directly to his or her former spouse, the parent is now required to bring cash or a certified check or money order to the clerk of the Family Court, who will then deposit the money and process it. If the money is not paid through the court on a timely basis, the Family Court will issue its own rule to show cause to hold the ex-spouse in contempt.

Obviously, if the payor spouse is hit by a truck and cannot work or is fired from his or her job, he or she probably will not be able to continue paying alimony in the original amount. A court can modify alimony based on a substantial change in circumstance, but the court will consider his or her earning capacity at that time. If, however, a spouse acts in bad faith to avoid paying what he or she owes, the courts will have no mercy. Voluntary changes in employment resulting in a lower income will be closely scrutinized (in child support cases, an even closer scrutiny is called for). See *Kelly v. Kelly*. Sometimes the facts are in dispute. In the traditional case, the husband claims he was demoted or his business is losing money, but the wife does not believe him. The courts closely scrutinize any voluntary change in employment and the Family Court has to decide who is right.

Retirement

Another area of contention is retirement. The courts have wrestled with this issue. On the one hand, the husband is entitled to retire. But of course, his income must decrease, and he must retire at a normal age, although we do not know exactly what that age is. Presumably a husband can retire at age sixty-five, although the Social Security Act now contemplates sixty-five to sixty-seven. On the other hand, can the husband retire early to spite the wife or to reduce his alimony payment?

The issue of retirement is an important issue, and anyone involved in a divorce needs good financial advice about his or her financial future. One or both parties will retire at some point. If the couple is affluent, they should share in private pension and retirement plans, IRAs, 401(k)s and military, civil service and state pension plans in the property division aspect of the case. The parties should also factor in Social Security, Medicare and assets available to provide for retirement.

Modification of Custody or Visitation

Raising children when one is divorced is sometimes extremely difficult, and custody and visitation arrangements do not always work. One problem with the system is that people anticipate how their custody and visitation arrangement will work before they have any experience with it. It is, therefore, not uncommon for people to find out that the arrangement to which they agreed is not necessarily the most workable.

Where the parties can agree, a custody and visitation agreement can be amended or modified after the divorce. And where the parties are not actually following the agreement but have informally changed it, it is best to write a new agreement and have a new order issued. The reason is obvious. One party or the other may change his or her mind later, and then demand that the parties go back to the original order as written.

Unfortunately, there is no easy way to change a custody or visitation order if the parties cannot agree. In order for the Family Court to modify a custody or visitation order, the moving party must show that there has been a material or substantial change of circumstance. Mere inconvenience will not suffice. The courts feel, rightly or wrongly, that once an order is issued, it ought to be obeyed and that litigants should not come back to court for any reason except those that are substantial. Thus, if a divorced mother is having boyfriends over at her house while the children are at home, or is involved with drugs, these activities could constitute a substantial change of circumstance allowing the court to change custody from the mother to the father. The fact that a child is not doing well in school, without more cause, is probably insufficient.

Litigants are frequently surprised to learn that what they regard as serious problems with their children may not amount to a "material" or "substantial" change of circumstance so as to justify a change in custody. This is all the more reason to get the custody and visitation provisions right the first time. Nevertheless, if one can prove that material or substantial changes of circumstance are affecting the welfare of the children, one can bring a new action in the Family Court to change custody. This is a new lawsuit altogether, complete with discovery, depositions, the appointment of a new guardian *ad litem* and a new trial. There is a heavy burden on the party seeking to change the custody order, and the evidence must, as a practical matter, be very convincing before a court will listen to it. The prevailing party can be awarded attorney's fees.

Litigants are frequently surprised to learn that what they regard as **serious problems with their children may not amount to a "material" or "substantial" change of circumstance** so as to justify a change in custody.

Modification of Support

The standard is the same with regard to support. A payee spouse can bring an action against the payor after a divorce to modify alimony if there has been a substantial change of circumstance that is unanticipated. Once again, this is difficult, because the mere fact that the payor's income has increased is not a basis to increase alimony. The fact that the payee's income has decreased is not necessarily a basis to decrease alimony. The Family Court frowns on undoing or changing an agreement that was entered into and approved by the court. A party seeking a change has the burden of proof. For example, unwarranted debts, inflation, an ex-wife's anticipated employment and "straightened financial situations" that are the normal consequences of most divorce are not changes of circumstance.

Where the wife had been working but was involved in a serious accident and can no longer work, this would normally constitute a change of circumstance authorizing the court to increase her alimony payments, provided the husband can afford to pay them. Or where the husband was fired from his job through no fault of his own or became ill and was no longer able to pay the alimony payments, this would also constitute a substantial change of circumstance.

Child support is always reviewable by the Family Court where there has been a material or substantial change in circumstances. The guidelines anticipate that child support will be recalculated from time to time as the income of the parties change. **Child support stands on a different plane than either custody or alimony.** The theory of alimony is that a former wife is entitled to live the lifestyle to which she was accustomed during her marriage. Therefore, any increase in the husband's income is irrelevant, because it has nothing to do with the lifestyle the parties lived during the marriage. On the other hand, child support is based on the concept that children are entitled to live the lifestyle that they could have had if their parents had stayed together. Therefore, any increase in the father's or mother's income would be a basis to change child support.

Children's needs change over the years, and whereas the child may have been attending a perfectly adequate school at the time of the divorce, the child may later experience problems and need to go to a private school. If the mother can show that the child needs these services and the father can afford to contribute to or pay them, the Family Court can modify the child support award to order him to do so. The same is true of health and medical issues. The classic case is when a child needs braces or orthodontic work and the father refuses to pay. The Family Court has the authority to order him to pay based on a change of circumstance.

Many mothers want to know whether or not they can withhold visitation when the ex-husband does not pay his child support, and many fathers want to know if they can withhold child support when the ex-wife refuses to allow him to visit with his child. The answer to both questions is a resounding "NO." Both parties are under an order to do certain things. If the ex-spouse fails to comply with an order, the remedy is to go to court for contempt. If an ex-wife withholds visitation, she is also liable for fees, contempt and an adjustment of the visitation schedule.

Many mothers want to know whether or not they can withhold visitation when the ex-husband does not pay his child support, and many fathers want to know if they can withhold child support when the ex-wife refuses to allow him to visit with his child. **The answer to both questions is a resounding "NO."**

The death of a former spouse can sometimes wreak havoc in the other spouse's life. As we have seen, in the traditional case, alimony terminates on the death of the payor. The payee likely was depending on the payor paying alimony for a certain number of years, or until his or her death. This is where the issue of life insurance becomes critical. Looking at the early death of a husband who is paying alimony, it would have behooved the wife to negotiate some provision for life insurance in the original agreement.

The death of a spouse also changes the custody arrangement. Some families find themselves in a very sad dilemma with the untimely death of a spouse. The law is very clear that a natural parent will have custody of minor children unless that parent is unfit to raise the child. Thus, a child who has been in the custody of a mother and a stepfather for many years, even where the stepfather has bonded with the child and even where the natural father is not an exemplary father, would be given to the custody of his or her natural father upon the death of the mother.

Appeals

Most of this book has been written under the assumption that the parties will have negotiated a settlement after some flurry of litigation. But there are cases where the parties litigate the matter to a final decision and then one party or the other appeals. Appellate law is a specialized area of the law with its own technical rules and procedures. After a trial and the issuance of a final order, one party may be dissatisfied. Typically, litigants will file a motion to amend the order, setting out how the judge has erred. If the judge made a mistake, it ought to be called to his or her attention so that it can be corrected. In general, judges do not grant motions to amend because they have already considered the issues when they issued the final order. Once the motion to amend has been ruled on, the dissatisfied party has thirty days to file a notice of appeal with the Court of Appeals.

A notice of appeal stays the ruling of the Family Court; the case is not over. If one party or the other is contesting the divorce itself, then the parties may not be divorced. All matters of property division are stayed (delayed until the appeal is over), meaning that the court's order that the husband transfer the marital home to the wife is stayed. The parties are in the same situation they were in at the beginning of the litigation with regard to division of property. Orders for custody, child support and alimony are not stayed. The same is true of custody determinations.

Parties in an appeal may file a petition for a writ of supersedeas. The dissatisfied party can ask the Court of Appeals to supercede, modify or change the order while the matter is pending appeal. While the Court of Appeals rarely grants such petitions, the court has in the past changed custody from the decision of the trial judge to the other parent pending a hearing on the appeal, and the court can change the amount or even the liability for alimony or child support.

The appellate process is long and slow. Attorneys order a copy of the transcript from the trial, and it may take the court reporter six months to type it. Upon receipt of the trial transcript, the lawyers have various periods of time to file briefs on the issues on appeal. The times for these filings are routinely extended. The matter is then studied by the Court of Appeals. From the time of a notice of appeal to the point when Court of Appeals issues an opinion can be anywhere from one to three years. Thus, the threat of appeal is a potent one in many cases.

Another potential legal problem is bankruptcy. This does not happen often, but people sometimes find themselves in poor financial circumstances as the marriage deteriorates, and husbands who are disgruntled with the result in Family Court resort to bankruptcy. It is critical to remember that the Bankruptcy Court is a federal court that takes precedence over any state court, including the Family Court. Thus, when a person files for bankruptcy, everything in the state system is stayed. The matter is in the hands of a bankruptcy judge. He or she can modify alimony or child support payments, stay any transfer of property and manage the bankrupt's estate according to the bankruptcy laws.

Sometimes bankruptcy judges will lower alimony amounts and child support amounts so as to allow the debtor to pay his debts. In recent years, however, Congress has recognized that the bankruptcy laws should not be used to thwart the orders of Family Courts. Thus, wives whose husbands have filed for bankruptcy have much more protection in the Bankruptcy Court. Unfortunately for the wife, Family Court attorneys are generally not specialists in the bankruptcy area, and specialized bankruptcy attorneys have to be retained to protect the wife's interest in the bankruptcy proceeding.

If the wife has any idea that the husband may file for bankruptcy, she ought to be certain that she receives the property agreed-upon free and clear of any liens, and to the extent the husband has promised to pay her money, that this debt is secured by a note and mortgage on real property. Secured debts are not dischargeable in bankruptcy.

Chapter 10

A Few Parting Words of Advice from a South Carolina Divorce Lawyer

> Love, the quest; Marriage the conquest; Divorce, the inquest.
>
> —Helen Rowland

These are some of the important lessons I have learned over the thirty-plus years I have practiced family law in South Carolina. First, if you have children, do not get a divorce. Divorce is very hard on the children, and no amount of rationalization will make that go away. My favorite critic of divorce, Barbara Dafoe Whitehead, wrote in *The Divorce Culture,*

> A mounting body of evidence from diverse and multiple sources shows that divorce has been a primary generator of new forms of inequality, disadvantage, and loss for American children. It has spawned a generation of angry and bereaved children who have a harder time learning, staying in school, and achieving at high levels.

Despite this advice, divorce is sometimes inevitable. It is thrust on people against their will, or there are circumstances that drive one spouse to leave the other. Divorce no longer stigmatizes anyone, and people rarely stay together solely for the sake of the children.

Set Realistic Goals

One of the most important pieces of advice I give clients is to set realistic goals. The Family Court does not have the ability to undo the wreck of your marriage, correct past injustices, award money or property that no longer exists, save children from parents or help you with your emotions. There are other resources for these tasks, namely friends, family, church, therapists, doctors and self-help books. The courts decide legal issues. Figure out what you can realistically accept: which property, how much support, what custody and visitation arrangements do you need? As Aristotle once said, "No wind is a fair wind if you do not know to which port you are sailing."

"Be Prepared" is the Boy Scout motto, and a pretty good divorce tip as well. Seek legal advice early, protect your assets and do not let your spouse sell the house or business. You can transfer money into your name a lot easier before litigation commences than afterward.

Help your lawyer help you. Organize papers and documents. Use e-mail, but remember it is not always confidential. Save up questions for one focused telephone call or meeting rather than calling your lawyer every day. Respect and work with the lawyer's paralegals and secretaries. Like nurses in hospitals, they have a lot of practical experience.

Going to trial is the last resort. It is expensive, stressful and unpredictable. Therefore, try your best to settle—but only after full financial disclosure, knowing your rights, thinking about your financial future (including life and health insurance, retirements, taxes, debts and liabilities as well as assets) and achieving a settlement you can live with.

There are four key players in every divorce: the husband, the wife, the husband's lawyer and the wife's lawyer. Any one of them can cause a train wreck. Apparently you made a mistake in selecting your spouse. Do not make another mistake in picking your lawyer. Take the time to find a lawyer who fits your case.

Do not be afraid of a trial or temporary hearing if the offer on the table is totally unacceptable. Where a husband refuses to pay alimony to a wife of twenty or thirty years who needs support, what does that wife have to lose by going to court? Some people really are unreasonable. A judge needs to tell these people what they are going to do. Settlement is usually the best option, but not if the deal is totally unfair.

Be completely truthful and honest with the Family Court. Once you have been caught in a lie, no one in the system will believe you.

Do not automatically assume your spouse is lying or trying to cheat you. Give him or her the chance to act honorably and do the right thing, even if you are hurt emotionally, suspicious or angry. Quick settlements are sometimes in everyone's best interest. Husbands who commit adultery and hurt their wives frequently agree to a more generous settlement at the beginning of the case, when they are feeling guilty, than at the end.

Do not be afraid of a trial or temporary hearing if the offer on the table is totally unacceptable.

Spouses who are unfamiliar with managing their finances need good advice on how to manage money. Unfortunately, there are a lot of unscrupulous "money managers" and "financial advisers."

Speak up. **Let your lawyer know what you want.** I once had a client who refused to settle or even participate in her divorce case. Her husband had left her for another woman, but she was morally and emotionally opposed to divorce. After months of explaining to her that her husband could get the divorce even if she refused to participate, I finally learned that what she wanted was to express in the legal documents and settlement agreement that she was opposed to the divorce and that it was proceeding only over her solemn objections. I wrote the agreement the way she wanted and the case ended. You may have an agenda, but if your lawyer does not know what it is, he or she cannot achieve the results you want.

Accept the inevitable. I often remind my clients of the first sentence of the serenity prayer: "God grant me the serenity to accept

the things I cannot change; courage to change the things I can; and the wisdom to know the difference." The law is what it is. The facts are what they are. I once tried a case because the husband would not accept the fact that his wife was entitled to half of his military pension. He told his lawyer, "When I was flying missions over Vietnam I didn't see her fat ass in the airplane with me." Inelegantly argued, I would agree, but nevertheless, an understandable emotion. Yet it is an emotion only, and not the law of the state of South Carolina. The husband had to accept the law that the wife contributed to his military pension even though she was not in the airplane with him.

A divorce has been likened to a death. As Elizabeth Kubler-Ross has pointed out, for the person who is left or rejected there is shock and denial, anger, depression, bargaining for the other spouse to return, sorrow and hopefully, eventually understanding and acceptance. The process sometimes has to unfold as it will. It cannot, at times, be shortened. For the person who left, the divorce is a business deal. For the rejected spouse, it is more like a natural disaster.

Avoid being the prosecutor and aggressor in court and explain to the judge how you have been hurt during the marriage. **Take the high road.** South Carolina judges are Southerners. They believe in courtesy and old-time values. They want you to talk about fairness and justice and what's best for the children. Accommodate your spouse on custody and visitation issues as much as possible, consistent with the well-being of your children. Remember, before the divorce, you probably were delighted for your spouse to spend more time with the children.

I have learned over the years that there are no good solutions to custody and visitation issues except for the parents working it out and getting along for the sake of the children. No "good" or "healthy" plan exists. Experts and judges do not know how to raise your children. The so-called experts do not know how to resolve custody and visitation disputes, and the best educated and smartest among them will tell you that reliable scientific or medical research on custody, visitation and the well-being of children is almost nonexistent. The

I have learned over the years that **there are no good solutions to custody and visitation issues except for the parents working it out** and getting along for the sake of the children.

only thing every expert and everyone in the Family Court system agree on is that *any* custodial arrangement will work if the parents agree on it and genuinely support it. If the parents can get along, the children do better. In high-conflict cases, the legal system has few options except to set out a custody/visitation schedule, enforce it by the contempt power and punish either or both parents who do not obey court orders. The parents, not the courts, destroy their children by continuing to fight.

Therapists: The Pros and Cons

Therapists, counselors, psychiatrists and psychologists are two-edged swords. Clearly therapy is helpful in many, if not most, divorce cases. I regularly recommend that clients seek counseling. However, there are dangers. *First, there is no real confidentiality in South Carolina when it comes to counseling or therapy.* There is no doctor-patient privilege in South Carolina. Everything you say to a psychiatrist, who is a medical doctor, is discoverable by the other side, a guardian *ad litem* or a judge. Psychiatrists can be forced to testify. As a practical matter, while there is a limited privilege for other mental health care professionals, they too can be forced to testify in custody cases and perhaps even in property division and alimony cases.

The Patient-Provider Records Act, §19-11-95 S.C. Code, sets forth a general rule prohibiting a "provider" from revealing the confidences of a patient who consults or is interviewed by the provider to diagnose, counsel or treat a mental illness or emotional condition. The term "provider" includes psychologists, professional counselors, associate counselors, marital and family therapists, master social workers and registered nurses who work in the field of mental health. The Patient-Provider Records Act does not apply to physicians or medical doctors. Even if your counselor or psychologist is protected by the Patient-Provider Records Act, the privilege established by the act is not absolute. The act specifically states that a "provider shall reveal confidences when required by statutory law or court order for good cause shown to the extent that the patient's care and treatment or the nature and extent of his mental illness or emotional condition are reasonably at issue in a proceeding." A party's care and treatment and the nature and extent of his or her mental illness or emotional condition are often at issue in the Family Court. Both the alimony statute and the Equitable Apportionment of Marital Property Act list criteria to determine alimony and property division, and both list the physical and emotional condition of each spouse as a criteria to be considered by the court. By making these claims, parties can place their mental condition at issue. A party's mental and emotional state is clearly relevant in a custody proceeding.

Thus, pick your therapist as carefully as you pick your lawyer. The same goes for a marriage counselor. While they may say they will never testify, they cannot give that assurance. When you are talking to them, you may very well be talking to your spouse, your spouse's lawyer or to the judge.

Respect the value system of the Family Court. The people who work in the system—judges, lawyers, clerks, secretaries, paralegals, experts, therapists, counselors, social workers—share a value system. They generally empathize with the party who is the victim. People do not feel sorry for greedy, angry litigants or those willing to lie to get their way. They resent parties who bully, threaten and do not respect the court or the law. They especially do not like disobedience of court orders. Saying negative things to the children about the other parent is a good way to lose your case.

Concentrate on the financial issues and do the boring and frustrating work necessary to resolve the case. The financial declaration is your roadmap to settling every issue except custody and visitation, and it even has an impact on that. Figuring out your true financial needs, your realistic income and expenses and valuing all assets and liabilities is your most important task. There is no substitute for a realistic budget. "Happiness," my banker Hugh Lane reminds me, "is a positive cash flow."

Spouses who are unfamiliar with managing their finances need good advice on how to manage money. Unfortunately, there are a lot of unscrupulous "money managers" and "financial advisers." Many divorce handbooks tout financial planners. Certainly certified financial planners (CFPs) have passed a lot of rigorous tests. I use planners or certified public accountants (CPAs) and tax lawyers I know. CPAs do not sell products such as stocks or life insurance. They are objective and bill by the hour for their advice. Get advice from your accountant, banker, financial planner, lawyer, friends and family.

Trust Your Lawyer

While this statement may appear self-serving, consider it carefully: trust your lawyer and look at the legal fees as a good investment in your future. One national handbook, *Divorce*, by Socrates Media, LLC, claims that "compromise and a mutually agreeable result are not the lawyer's primary goals." This is pure, unadulterated hogwash. The great majority of lawyers are interested in settlement. Indeed, it is not unusual for some clients to feel that their lawyer is not willing to "fight for them." Of course, there are some lawyers who cause more problems than they solve, but the same can be said for mediators, counselors and judges. By and large, the domestic relations bar in South Carolina is dedicated to the amicable resolution of divorce cases.

One of my favorite stories about attorney's fees involved the legendary attorney "Spot" Mazingo from Darlington, who (the story goes) was asked by a client to get something important done in Columbia involving the state government. The service was extremely valuable to the client. No fee arrangement had been made in advance. The client received a bill from Mr. Mazingo for $50,000 (this was in the 1960s). The client was outraged at the amount of the bill and called and demanded that Mr. Mazingo itemize the bill. He graciously replied that he would be happy to do so, and then sent the following bill:

Making telephone call to person in Columbia:	1.0 hour	$ 200
Knowing who to call:		$49,800

There is a lot of wisdom in this story. One can hire a lawyer who is not particularly competent at a lower hourly rate, achieve a bad result and save a great deal of money in attorney's fees. Or one can hire an attorney who knows what he or she is doing and pay them more, but receive a far better result. The key, of course, is to find the right lawyer at the right price for your case. **The most expensive lawyer is not necessarily the best lawyer.** But then neither is the least expensive lawyer. The best way to find a lawyer is to talk to people who have had cases similar to yours and ask whether they were happy with their lawyer's services. Or ask people who you trust (friends, business associates or attorneys) who the best lawyer for your case would be. Lawyers rate other lawyers in a publication called *Martindale-Hubbell*, which is available at www.martindale.com or at the local library. Another publication worth consulting is *Best Lawyers in America* at www.bestlawyers.com and the websites of the American Bar Association (www.abanet.org) and the American Academy of

Spouses who are unfamiliar with managing their finances need good advice on how to manage money. Unfortunately, there are a lot of unscrupulous "money managers" and "financial advisers."

Matrimonial Lawyers (www.aaml.com is the website for the national group and www.bestdivorcelawyers-sc.com is the website for the American Academy's South Carolina chapter of divorce attorneys).

The same advice I have given about lawyers, i.e., find the right one for your case, also applies to experts. Real estate and personal property appraisers, CPAs and business valuations come in many flavors. Spend the money to hire effective experts. Your house, other real estate, a business, artwork or collectibles can sometimes make a huge difference in the value of a case. Spending thousands of dollars to gain tens of thousands or hundreds of thousands makes good business sense.

While everyone says that you should not let your emotions govern your actions in Family Court, the fact of the matter is that this is easier said than done. Nevertheless, one way of thinking about it is to let your therapist handle your emotional problems and let your lawyer handle your legal problems. Despite all of the emotions—which are definitely understandable—a divorce case is, at bottom, a legal and a business decision. It is the dissolution of a legal partnership that has assets and income, and neither the Family Court nor any lawyer can make things perfectly right; nor can they easily solve the emotional problems that often crop up. The Family Court is like the emergency room at a hospital, and the lawyers and judges are like emergency room doctors. They cannot go back in time and change what has happened. All they can do is treat the injury they have in front of them. If you have realistic expectations of how the system works and what it can do, you will not be disappointed.

Table of Cases

Table of Cases

Notes

Chapter 2

1. *Thompson v. Thompson*, 10 Rich Eq. 416 (1859).

Chapter 3

1. *Beasley v. Beasley*, 216 S.E.2d 535 (1975); *Johnson v. Johnson*, 372 S.E.2d 107 (Ct. App. 1988), cert. denied 298 S.C. 117 (1989); *O'Neill v. O'Neill*, 359 S.E.2d 68 (Ct. App. 1987).

2. Adultery presently does not bar alimony after either (1) the formal signing of a property or settlement agreement or (2) the entry of a permanent order of separate maintenance and support or a permanent order approving a property settlement, S.C. Code Ann. 20-3-130 (A). A bill is pending in the General Assembly (which has passed the Senate and is now in the House of Representatives) that would abolish the absolute bar to alimony and change the law by allowing the court to consider whether the spouse seeking alimony and support has not engaged in adultery and that the other spouse has engaged in adultery prior to the signing of a property settlement agreement or the entry of a permanent order relating to support. The bill adds, "The degree of additional weight given by the court to the award or the amount of the award of alimony or separate maintenance and support must be in the court's discretion." The bill is S196 and was referred to the House Judiciary Committee on February 20, 2007. The bill can be found at www.scstatehouse.net.

3. This very simple example ignores further tax savings the wife may receive if she has dependency exemptions and a mortgage payment, for example.

Chapter 4

1. See for example, *Barr v. Barr*, 336 S.E.2d 481 (Ct. App. 1985).

2. *R.G.M. v. D.G.M.*, 410 S.E.2d 564 (1991); *Reid v. Reid*, 383 S.E.2d 724 (Ct. App. 1984); *Kirsch v. Kirsch*, 383 S.E.2d 724 (Ct. App 1989); *Brandi v. Brandi*, 396 S.E.2d 124 (Ct. App. 1990).